TERRORISM IN THE WEST 2008

A Guide to Terrorism Events and Landmark Cases

Daveed Gartenstein-Ross
Joshua D. Goodman
Laura Grossman

FDD PRESS
A Division of the
FOUNDATION FOR DEFENSE OF DEMOCRACIES
Washington, D.C.

For information about permission to reproduce selections from
this monograph, write to:
ctr@defenddemocracy.org, or Permissions, FDD Press, P.O.
Box 33249, Washington, D.C. 20033

ISBN: 978-0-9819712-2-3

FDD Press
P.O. Box 33249
Washington, D.C. 20033

Cover photo credit: Unai Beroiz/EPA/Corbis

CONTENTS

SECTION III.
Landmark Cases *67*

ACKNOWLEDGMENTS

We would like to acknowledge our colleagues at the Center for Terrorism Research, both past and present, who contributed to the substantial research that supported this project. We owe a debt of gratitude to Katie Ake, Joanne Darlington, Nathan Hitchen, Joshua Kaplan, Adam Ptashkin, and Cindy Tan; and to Sara Westfall for her excellent work on layout and design. We extend our thanks to Clifford D. May and Mark Dubowitz, the president and executive director at Foundation for Defense of Democracies respectively, for supporting our work.

We appreciate the valuable additions to the report by contributors Jeff Breinholt, Douglas Farah, Rohan Gunaratna, Andrew C. McCarthy, and Reuven Paz. Their unique perspectives and expertise on the subject matter should significantly enhance the reader's understanding of major trends and developments in terrorism in 2008.

Last but not least, we would like to thank The Bodman Foundation, The Lynde and Harry Bradley Foundation, and The Kathryn W. Davis Foundation, whose generous support made this project possible.

ACRONYMS

ACLU	American Civil Liberties Union (U.S.)
AQIM	al Qaeda in the Islamic Maghreb
CIA	Central Intelligence Agency (U.S.)
CPS	Crown Prosecution Service (U.K.)
CSIS	Canadian Security Intelligence Service
DEA	Drug Enforcement Administration (U.S.)
DST	Direction de la Surveillance du Territoire (France)
ELA	Revolutionary People's Struggle
ELF	Earth Liberation Front
ETA	Euskadi Ta Askatasuna
EU	European Union
FARC	Revolutionary Armed Forces of Colombia
FBI	Federal Bureau of Investigations (U.S.)
FISA	Foreign Intelligence Surveillance Act (U.S.)
GICM	Moroccan Islamic Combatant Group
GIMF	Global Islamic Media Front
HLF	Holy Land Foundation
HMTD	Hexamethylene Triperozide Diamine
IJU	Islamic Jihad Union
IMU	Islamic Movement of Uzbekistan
IRA	Irish Republican Army
LTTE	Liberation Tigers of Tamil Eelam
NATO	North Atlantic Treaty Organization
PKK	Kurdistan Workers' Party
PST	Politiets Sikkerhetsjeneste (Norway)
RAW	Research & Intelligence Wing (India)
RUF	Revolutionary United Front (Sierra Leone)
TATP	Triacetone Triperoxide
TFG	Transitional Federal Government (Somalia)

SECTION I.
ASSESSING TRENDS IN TERRORISM IN THE WEST

Terrorism is not a new phenomenon, nor is it likely to disappear anytime soon. It is not the exclusive domain of any single religion or ideology, nor do all terrorists come from the same socioeconomic class or share the same mental pathologies.[1] In part, the diversity within contemporary terrorism is what makes it so great a challenge. This report describes, in great detail, the state of terrorism in Western countries over the course of 2008.[2]

Before turning to terrorism events in the West during 2008 and key developments within Western countries' legal systems, we are going to pinpoint a few broad trends—a few currents that run through the various incidents and cases that follow.

The Nexus of Crime and Terrorism

In 2008, we saw the connections between transnational crime and terrorism deepen.[3] The linkage between the two is not a new

---

1. On these points, see Marc Sageman, *Understanding Terror Networks* (Philadelphia: University of Pennsylvania Press, 2004); Marc Sageman, *Leaderless Jihad: Terror Networks in the Twenty-First Century* (Philadelphia: University of Pennsylvania Press, 2008).
2. The countries examined in this study are those that comprise the European Union, as well as Australia, Canada, Norway, and the United States.
3. For an in-depth examination of the connection between transnational crime and terrorism, see Daveed Gartenstein-Ross & Kyle Dabruzzi, *The Convergence of Crime and Terror: Law Enforcement Opportunities and Perils* (New York: Manhattan Institute Center for Policing Terrorism, 2007).

phenomenon: the USSR had been a major sponsor of terrorist and insurgent groups during the Cold War, and after the Soviet Union's collapse, these groups were forced to look elsewhere financially. Many turned to criminal activities, such as the drug trade.

There are two strategically significant aspects of terrorist involvement in criminal activity. First, it allows terrorists to gain financially while damaging the societies they target. Second, law enforcement can derive some advantage from the crime-terrorism nexus by shutting down terrorists through targeting their criminal activities. This approach echoes the strategy used to fight the mob in the early to mid-twentieth century, as typified by the prosecution of Al Capone.[4] Though Capone's litany of offenses included murder, bribery, and running illegal breweries, the government would have had trouble proving his guilt beyond a reasonable doubt for his most notorious activities. Instead, Capone was charged with tax evasion, prompting the incredulous mobster to say, "The government can't collect legal taxes from illegal money."[5] Capone proved to be mistaken, and he entered an Atlanta prison on May 5, 1932. Shortly after 9/11, then-attorney general John Ashcroft publicly advocated an Al Capone/mob model for prosecuting suspected terrorists, shutting them down by charging them for their full range of violations of the law (rather than just their terrorist activities).[6]

As this report will show, concerns about the contemporary connection between criminal activities and terrorism are clear in Bulgaria, a country rife with organized crime. An April 2008 parliamentary report charged that profits from the country's drug trade were channeled to Middle Eastern terrorist groups.

In the U.S., one individual, Khan Mohammed, was convicted of narcotics distribution and narcoterrorism for his role in financing Taliban activities through the drug trade. But the 2008 newsmaker who best exemplified the crime/terror nexus was Viktor Bout, the world's leading arms trafficker. He was arrested at a Bangkok hotel while

---

4. For background on Al Capone and his prosecution, see Laurence Bergreen, *Capone: The Man and the Era* (New York: Simon & Schuster, 1994) and John Kobler, *Capone: The Life and World of Al Capone* (New York: Da Capo Press, 1971).
5. Daniel C. Richman & William J. Stuntz, "Al Capone's Revenge: An Essay on the Political Economy of Pretextual Prosecution," *Columbia Law Review*, 2005, pp. 583-84.
6. Attorney General John Ashcroft, "Prepared Remarks for the U.S. Mayors Conference," Oct. 25, 2001.

attempting to buy weapons for the narcoterrorist group Revolutionary Armed Forces of Colombia (FARC). Bout, as a "shadow facilitator," was able to provide critical services to terrorist organizations and organized crime, as well as legitimate state actors.

Moreover, prosecutors employed the tactic of "undercharging," charging defendants with lesser crimes than terrorism offenses, in at least two cases. In Australia, Jack Thomas, a.k.a. "Jihad Jack," was convicted of possessing a falsified passport after prosecutors failed to convict him on terrorism charges. Similarly, prosecutors in the U.S. managed to win convictions against three former Care International officers for engaging in a scheme to conceal material facts from the U.S. and conspiring to defraud the government, despite the organization's suspected involvement in jihadist activity.

Transnational Terrorist Groups Develop Capabilities in the West

Transnational terrorist groups have continued to develop significant capacities in the West in order to build their operational strength and resiliency. The Kurdish Workers Party (PKK), Liberation Tigers of Tamil Eelam (LTTE), Hizballah, Islamic Movement of Uzbekistan (IMU), and al-Qaeda in the Islamic Maghreb (AQIM) were all active in the West in 2008.

When transnational terrorist groups operate in the West to build their capacities and resilience, they often do not intend to carry out attacks on Western soil. Rather, Western countries can be used as bases to raise funds (often illegally), obtain equipment for the organization's use, and propagandize. Various countries' legal regimes will have an impact on terrorist groups' ability to accomplish this, with European countries often more permissive than the United States. As this report notes, the LTTE experienced a dramatic military defeat in 2009, and if the terrorist group is able to make a comeback, the networks it has built in the West will likely be a part of that story.

The Threat Posed by Islamic Terrorism

In 2008, Islamic-inspired terrorism remained the most serious terrorist threat faced by Western countries. This is true due to a mix of motivations and capabilities. Put simply, at present only the Islamic terrorist movement possesses both the desire to do major damage to Western interests, and the capacity to turn this desire into reality.

One advantage that Islamic terrorists have is access to territorial safe havens. The 9-11 Commission concluded that to carry out catastrophic acts of terror, terrorist groups require sanctuaries that provide them with "time, space, and ability to perform competent planning and staff work," as well as "opportunities and space to recruit, train, and select operatives with the needed skills and dedication."[7] Following the U.S.'s 2001 invasion of Afghanistan, al-Qaeda and aligned jihadist groups found new safe havens. As of 2008, the two major safe havens enjoyed by violent Islamist groups were in Pakistan and Somalia. Consequently, terrorist activity with linkages to both countries could be glimpsed frequently in 2008—in Germany, Norway, Sweden, the U.S., and elsewhere.

Unless there are significant political and strategic changes, there will likely be a number of future plots with connections to Pakistan and Somalia. Moreover, plots with connections to one of these countries may be more ambitious in scale due to the advantages afforded by geographic safe havens.

Balancing Security and Civil Liberties

As Western governments try to protect their citizens from the threat of terrorism, there has been continued controversy about how best to strike a balance between security and civil liberties. This manifested itself in various ways during 2008. In Canada, lawyers for Mohammad Mahjoub, who was suspected of belonging to a group closely linked to al-Qaeda, responded with outrage when they learned that the Canadian Security Intelligence Service (CSIS) had listened in on calls with their client.[8] In France, public controversy erupted over the creation of a new security database called Edvige, which was designed to collect personal information on persons deemed to be possible threats to the public order by the Interior Ministry.[9] Opponents collected around 130,000 signatures opposing the database, and French president Nicolas Sarkozy retooled Edvige as a result of the outcry.[10] The British use of wiretapping has led critics to charge

---

7. *The 9-11 Commission Report: Final Report of the National Commission on Terrorist Attacks Upon the United States* (New York: W.W. Norton Co., 2004), pp. 60-61.
8. "CSIS Stops Tapping Calls Between Lawyers, Terrorism Suspects," *CBC News* (Canada), Dec. 23, 2008.
9. Samuel Laurent, "Edvige: Ce Qui Inquiète," *Le Figaro* (France), Sept. 8, 2008.
10. Emma Jane Kirby, "Sarkozy in Civil Liberties U-Turn," *BBC News,* Sept. 10, 2008.

that the country has become "a surveillance state,"[11] and a May 2008 British Home Office proposal to expand authorities' ability to access records of telephone calls, e-mails, text messages, and Internet logs ran into a firestorm of criticism. There was also furious debate over governmental surveillance in the United States.

The question of how to find the best balance between security and civil liberties will not go away anytime soon. Andrew C. McCarthy, whose distinguished legal career includes the successful prosecution of Sheikh Omar Abdel Rahman and eleven others in connection with the 1993 World Trade Center bombing and a plot to bomb New York City landmarks, weighs in with one perspective on surveillance.

Surveillance Round-Up
By Andrew C. McCarthy

Last July, President Bush signed the FISA Amendments Act of 2008, substantially ending an extensive debate over national security surveillance law. The controversy sprang to life in December 2005, when the *New York Times* disclosed that the government had been conducting warrantless electronic monitoring, targeting international communications into and out of the United States.

Thirty years earlier, in 1978, Congress had enacted FISA, the Foreign Intelligence Surveillance Act, in order to provide Americans with a modicum of due process protection from wiretapping done not for criminal investigative purposes (for which a judicial warrant is required) but for national-security purposes against foreign threats (for which warrants were not required). FISA, an overreaction to Nixon-era domestic spying abuses, was both constitutionally suspect and operationally impractical. Suspect because intelligence collection, particularly in wartime, is an executive branch responsibility, yet FISA purports to vest responsibility for it in the judiciary, which is neither institutionally competent for the task nor politically accountable to the Americans whose lives are at stake. Impractical because the statute was written for 1970s telephony and thus became increasingly difficult to apply as telecom technology revolutionized in the ensuing three decades. That challenge, though daunting, is only part of the practicality problem. There is also the

---

11. See "Bugging on the Rise in Britain," *Daily Telegraph* (London), Jan. 30, 2008.

peril flowing from the mismatch between a national security mission and law-enforcement tools.

Probable cause judicial warrants are required in criminal investigations where the police have a veritable monopoly on the use of force, there is no strategic threat to the nation, and investigators are seeking evidence of a completed or ongoing crime from Americans presumed innocent. They are a poor fit when our country is threatened by rogue nations and foreign terror networks, the government is seeking not evidence but intelligence, and the object is not to prove past crimes but to prevent future acts of aggression and terrorism. When the government has "probable cause," it already knows someone is potentially dangerous; the task in confronting secretive, transnational terror networks that embed operatives to roam among us is to figure out who may be dangerous.

The escape hatch from FISA's unintended consequences has always been presidential power. Ever since FISA's enactment, administrations of both parties have taken the position that the legislation cannot trump the commander-in-chief's authority under the Constitution's Article I to protect the nation. In fact, in 1994, when FISA was expanded by Congress to cover physical searches (after President Clinton had authorized warrantless searches in a national security investigation), the Clinton Justice Department took the firm position that the amendment did not override the president's inherent authority to authorize searches in a national emergency. ("It is important to understand," explained Deputy Attorney General Jamie Gorelick in congressional testimony, "that the rules and methodology for criminal searches are inconsistent with the collection of foreign intelligence and would *unduly frustrate the president in carrying out his foreign intelligence responsibilities*.") The Carter Justice Department had taken the same position when FISA was first enacted. Since then, every federal appellate court to consider the constitutionality of FISA has agreed, including the Foreign Intelligence Court of Review (the specialized appellate court created by Congress to review FISA questions), which reaffirmed in 2002, after nearly a quarter century of FISA's operation, that presidents maintain inherent constitutional authority despite the terms of FISA.

It should not have required a corpus of national security

law or the specter of Mohammed Atta receiving orders from his overseas terror masters to grasp why this is so. The surveillance effort targeted cross-border communications. The Supreme Court has long held that border security is a core ingredient of sovereignty, and thus that its management is a core responsibility of the political branches, not federal judges. Warrants, thus, are not required to conduct highly intrusive physical searches of even American citizens and their belongings as they enter or leave our country. There is no constitutional privacy right against warrantless searches of cross-border mailings, or of the contents (including stored e-mail) of a computer being carried across national boundaries.

Similarly, Americans have no legitimate expectation of privacy when their communications pass outside the United States, where American law does not apply and both foreign intelligence services and international terror networks seek to intercept them. (Under the view of libertarian extremists, only the American intelligence community would be cut off from such intelligence—in a time of war against a transnational terror network that has already demonstrated its capacity to conduct sneak mass-murder attacks in our homeland.) Moreover, the law has long recognized the government's authority to conduct warrantless searches in circumstances regarded as "exigent" even though they pale in comparison to the national security threats posed by war and terrorism.

Every wartime president since the Civil War had authorized warrantless surveillance inside the United States, but the revelation that Bush had done so sparked a political firestorm—notwithstanding that senior members of Congress had been briefed throughout the existence of the effort, which was known as the "Terrorist Surveillance Program." Though there were compelling legal arguments to support its legality, the program was brought under the supervision of the FISA court in 2007. The details are classified, but Bush administration officials publicly asserted that the program's effectiveness had not been compromised, suggesting that the FISA court has accepted a legal theory under which judges authorize blocks of surveillance orders on an anticipatory basis, with monitoring triggered upon connection of a new target to communications facilities used by known terror networks. This is helpful, but far from perfect: It does not help, for example, with previously unknown terror groups.

Finally, the 2008 legislation cured two severe problems. First, it gave immunity from suit to telecom companies that had assisted the warrantless program based on executive branch assurances of its legality. Our nation's ability to maintain a technological edge over America's technologically adept enemies hinges on the continued cooperation of the nation's top telecommunications experts—cooperation that would be lost if the telecoms came to see it as fraught with potential billions in liability.

Second, the act clarified that communications occurring wholly outside the U.S. (e.g., a call from Pakistan to Afghanistan) continue to fall outside the coverage of FISA, and thus outside court supervision. Such foreign-to-foreign communications were excluded from coverage under the original FISA but had been held by the FISA court to require warrants—due to digital-age technology developments which now route communication bits through American networks even if all interlocutors were foreigners and were physically located outside the U.S. (i.e., in places where U.S. court jurisdiction does not extend). That ruling threatened to paralyze American foreign intelligence collection. Its effective reversal by statute was urgently needed.

When Does Speech Cross the Line?

One area where the conflict between security and civil liberties can be glimpsed is the question of when speech has crossed the line to illegal support for, or encouragement of, terrorism. In 2008, there were several arrests and convictions of individuals for propagandizing on behalf of terrorist groups. In Germany, two men were arrested for operating a jihadist web site that prosecutors charge was designed "to reach the largest possible audience with propaganda that serves to mobilize more supporters and intimidate the western public," and another man was convicted of terrorist solicitation and recruitment due to his propaganda efforts. In Spain, three men were arrested for "promoting radical ideology among the Muslim community," while a married U.K. couple was charged with distributing propaganda.

A significant appellate court case in Britain involved five

young Muslim students who had been convicted in late 2007 "for downloading and sharing extremist terrorism-related material." In overturning the convictions, the court held that for possession of terrorism-related material to constitute a prosecutable offense, there had to be a reasonable suspicion that the material was connected to an actual terrorist act. The solicitor for one of the accused expressed concern that prior to this judgment, young Muslims "could have been prosecuted … for simply looking at any material on the basis that it might be connected in some way to terrorist purposes."

Just as controversies about surveillance will be with us for a long time, so too will controversies about when speech crosses the line. Courts will confront similar questions for years to come.

Terrorism Aimed at Free Speech

Free speech is threatened not only by overzealous prosecutions, but also by terrorist activity. This has been evident for years: the possibility of a terrorist attack against author Salman Rushdie was one of the concerns that drove him underground when Ayatollah Khomeini issued a *fatwa* condemning him to death for the publication of his novel *The Satanic Verses*. Dutch filmmaker Theo van Gogh was killed in a particularly vicious attack following the release of his controversial film *Submission*. And after Danish newspaper *Jyllands-Posten* published twelve cartoons caricaturing the Prophet Muhammad in 2005, there were violent protests in many corners of the world, and the cartoonists and the newspaper's culture editor were threatened.[12]

In 2008, three men were arrested in Britain after plotting attacks against the publisher of the controversial novel *The Jewel of Medina*, by American author Sherry Jones. (Her novel was a historical romance that followed the life of Muhammad's young wife Aisha.) Ultimately Jones's publisher, Random House, dropped the title prior to publication due to fears of threats. The threat of violence may put pressure on people's ability to engage in free expression on certain issues in the future.

Terrorist Copycatting

In 2008, there were several cases of what can be described as

---

12. For more on how threats of violence can be used to suppress speech, see Daveed Gartenstein-Ross, "The Freedoms We Fight For," *Weekly Standard Online*, Nov. 28, 2005.

terrorist copycatting. In Britain, a man named Malcolm Hodges had a "festering grudge" against several accounting organizations due to his failure to pass a qualifying exam in the 1990s. He pled guilty to recklessly encouraging terrorism after sending letters to several mosques encouraging attacks against these institutions, which he claimed embodied "the corrupt and Western society which are abhorrent to true believers." Also, a Wisconsin resident named Jake Brahm pled guilty to willfully conveying false information through hoax Internet threats he made about simultaneous dirty bomb attacks on seven different American cities.

In part, these copycatting incidents show how terrorism has captured the public imagination. Deep unhappiness with various accounting bodies, the juvenile desire to stir things up and get attention—both resulted in reaching for the terrorist card in some capacity. People who engage in terrorist copycatting clearly believe that terrorism works: they believe that it gets attention, scares people. Hodges apparently had such a strong belief that terrorism works that he felt sending anonymous letters to a handful of mosques might actually incite people to violence.

Suicide Bombings

Suicide bombings are of both symbolic and strategic importance to terrorist organizations.[13] In 2008, two Western countries—Germany and the U.S.— saw their own citizens die as suicide bombers for the first time. There were also suicide plots uncovered in Belgium, Spain, and the U.K. Many trends can only be discerned over the course of years. It will be important to watch whether suicide bombings continue to occur more frequently in the West.

Is Violence Becoming Normalized as a Form of Protest?

One unfortunate emerging trend may be the normalization of terrorist acts as a form of political or social protest. Following bombings that targeted gas pipelines operated by Canadian company EnCana, one observer noted that such attacks are "almost like the price of doing business." One question that Western societies must confront is whether some segments of the population increasingly accept that violence is a justifiable response to views or actions with which they

---

13. See Robert Pape, *Dying to Win: The Strategic Logic of Suicide Terrorism* (New York: Random House, 2005).

strongly disagree. Whether the despised actor against which violence is aimed is a company operating gas pipelines, a researcher whose experiments include animals, an abortion provider, or the publisher of a book perceived as offensive, violence as a routine response to disagreements has a corrosive effect on society.

The classical liberal principles upon which Western society was built favor debate, discussion, and mediation among competing interests as a means of settling disagreement. What happens to public discourse and these key principles when taking a position or action unpopular with some group becomes dangerous? Is the resort to violence within Western societies as a means of advancing one's preferred outcomes increasing? And if so, how can policymakers, public intellectuals, and others help to underscore that using violence in such circumstances is not acceptable for civilized people?

If terrorism is indeed being normalized as a form of political or social protest, one question we must confront is whether it will grow more deadly over time. While acts of "ecotage" may indeed be "the price of doing business" for companies whose activities have an environmental cost, will these acts evolve from targeting company equipment to targeting people? In late 2008, a crudely constructed bomb was left outside the offices of Shell Ireland to protest a gas pipeline project in Co Mayo. Following this, a spokesman for Shell Ireland told the press:

> We've had a lot of attacks in Mayo. There has [been] fencing torn down, there has been arson attacks. We have had guys reversing through the gates. This is a sinister development and very serious escalation. This is another notch up and we're extremely worried.

Many terrorist groups have escalated their actions over time. Al-Qaeda's militant activities, for example, grew to an attack on American soil that killed almost 3,000 people, and less than two years later the group sought and obtained a *fatwa* for terrorism against the United States employing weapons of mass destruction.[14] If groups that have chosen to employ violence as a means of advancing their social and political goals do not feel that they have achieved their desired results, will they become more violent? Will their attacks evolve from property

---

14. See Nasir bin Hamd al-Fahd, "A Treatise on the Legal Status of Using Weapons of Mass Destruction Against Infidels," May 2003.

damage to injuring humans, and eventually to killing them?

As previously noted, trends can only be discerned over time, and it is too early to say that there is a widespread trend toward the escalation of terrorist violence across multiple countries. However, there were several disturbing data points during 2008.

SECTION II.
TERRORISM EVENTS

This section provides a comprehensive look at terrorism events in the West over the course of 2008. Events are defined as successful attacks, disrupted or failed plots, and arrests for anything legally defined as terrorist activity in the country of study.

BELGIUM

Though Belgium is traditionally considered one of Europe's most liberal societies, this liberalism has not shielded the country from terrorist presence and plots. Since 9/11, Belgian authorities have uncovered and arrested an array of terrorists. For example, nearly two dozen men alleged to be affiliated with al-Qaeda were tried in Belgium in 2003. The lead suspect, former professional soccer player Nizar Trabelsi, was convicted of "plotting to blow up a military base used by U.S. forces in Belgium," while Tunisian-born Tarek Maaroufi was convicted "for his involvement in the 2001 assassination of an anti-Taliban military commander in Afghanistan."[15] Another example is the "Maaseik network," centered around the small town of Maaseik, which was linked to both the Moroccan Islamic Combatant Group (GICM) and the insurgency in Iraq. A 2007 report notes that although this network "did not plan a terrorist attack on Belgian soil, they formed a well

---

15. Jarrett Murphy, "Terror Verdict for Soccer Pro," *CBS News*, Sept. 30, 2003.

organized logistical support cell, providing for false papers, hideouts, etc."[16]

The major counterterrorism action in Belgium came in late 2008, on the eve of the European Union's summit in Brussels. In a series of raids, police arrested fourteen people of Moroccan descent. A Belgian police source explained to CNN that one of these individuals "was planning to carry out a suicide attack in Belgium," and that the individuals arrested "had contacts at the 'highest levels of al Qaeda.'"[17] The source told the news network that the police "had only 24 hours to act."[18] Among the pieces of information leading authorities to this conclusion was a police intercept on December 7 in which members of the group discussed whether women and children should be evacuated.[19]

On December 12, the day after the arrests, eight of the suspects were released "after a judge ruled that there was insufficient evidence to keep them in detention."[20] Six of the individuals were charged, and federal prosecutor Johan Delmulle claimed that the would-be suicide bomber "had been given the go-ahead for the attack and had already said good-bye to his family."[21]

Among those arrested and detained was Malika el-Aroud, the widow of one of the two assassins of Northern Alliance leader Ahmed Shah Massoud. Known as an "al-Qaeda living legend," el-Aroud "calls herself a female warrior for Al Qaeda and writes jihadist screeds on the internet under the name Oum Obeyda."[22] El-Aroud's second husband,

16. Rik Coolsaet & Tanguy Struye de Swielande, *Belgium and Counterterrorism Policy in the Jihadi Era (1986-2007)* (Brussels: Egmont Royal Institute for International Relations, 2007), p. 8.

17. "Belgian Police Arrest 'Al Qaeda Legend,'" *CNN*, Dec. 11, 2008.

18. Ibid.

19. Helen Warrell, "Al-Qaeda Suspects Arrested in Belgian Raids," *Financial Times*, Dec. 11, 2008.

20. Huma Yusuf, "Belgium Charges Six with Connections to a Terrorist Group," *Christian Science Monitor*, Dec. 12, 2008.

21. "Belgium Detains al-Qaeda Suspects," *BBC News*, Dec. 12, 2008.

22. Steven Erlanger, "14 Arrested in Belgium for Links to Terrorism," *New York Times*, Dec. 11, 2008. The *New York Times* published an interesting profile of her in May 2008. See Elaine Sciolino & Souad Mekhennet, "Al Qaeda Warrior Uses Internet to Rally Women," *New York Times*, May 28, 2008.

Moez Garsalloui, was also believed to be among those arrested.[23]

Most of the fourteen individuals arrested in the sweep had Belgian passports, and police said that "[t]hree of the suspects had traveled to the Afghanistan-Pakistan border region to participate in fighting or training camps."[24]

BULGARIA

Bulgaria, with a population of 7.7 million, has little history, and few incidents, of religiously-inspired terrorism. It is, however, one of the most corrupt nations in the EU,[25] and organized crime poses a particular challenge.[26]

The prevalence of crime within Bulgaria has created a space in which some terrorist fundraising can occur. An April 2008 parliamentary report examining Interior Ministry corruption found "high-level involvement with organised crime."[27] Examples included government secrets that "were leaked to mafia figures involved in drug trafficking," and a senior minister's frequent meetings with underworld bosses. Directly relevant to the connection between crime and terrorism in Bulgaria, the report charged that profits from the country's drug trade were channeled to Middle Eastern terrorist groups. The MPs' report said: "Bulgarian crime groups engaged in trafficking … drugs sometimes work together with Arab citizens linked to terrorist organisations."[28]

23. Erlanger, "14 Arrested in Belgium for Links to Terrorism."
        Proceedings in this case continued in 2009. On January 7, 2009, the court held a closed session in which it examined the warrants for the six remaining suspects. "Les Six Terroristes Présumés Devant la Chambre du Conseil," *Info RTBF* (Belgium), Jan. 7, 2009. One of them, Jean Trefois—who is described as an extremist convert to Islam—was released. "Brusselse Terrorismeverdachte Vrijgelaten," *DeMorgen* (Belgium), Jan. 7, 2009.
24. "Belgian Police Arrest 'Al Qaeda Legend,'" *CNN*.
25. Doreen Carvajal & Stephen Castle, "Bulgarian Corruption Troubling EU," *New York Times*, Oct. 15, 2008.
26. Bureau of International Narcotics and Law Enforcement Affairs, *International Narcotics Control Strategy Report* (2007).
27. David Charter, "Organised Crime Link to Islamic Terror Exposed," *Times* (London), Apr. 10, 2008.
28. Ibid. See also "Terrorist Groups 'Funded by Bulgaria Drugs,'" *Balkan Insight*, Apr. 9, 2008.

CANADA

While no religiously-motivated terrorist plot has succeeded in Canada in recent years, a number of plots have been uncovered. Moreover, there have been instances of ecoterrorism targeting Canada's oil and gas industry. Ecoterrorist strikes against the Canadian oil industry were the country's most notable terrorist incidents in 2008.

Ecoterrorism Strikes Canadian Oil

Over the course of 2008, there were three bombings of EnCana-owned gas pipelines.[29] The first blast, which occurred on October 12 near the British Columbia-Alberta border, produced a two-meter crater under a pipeline close to Tomslake. It was preceded by three letters mailed to media outlets with threatening handwritten messages demanding that EnCana end its Tomslake operations.[30] One letter, which was sent to the *Dawson Creek Daily News*, stated: "We will no longer negotiate with terrorists which you are as you keep endangering our families with crazy expansion of deadly gas wells in our home lands."[31]

An EnCana vice president issued a statement directly addressing the perpetrators: "Your actions have imperiled your fellow citizens, EnCana employees, and emergency response personnel. We do not believe you intend the loss of life, but you must understand that a continuation of the bombings dramatically raises the danger of that occurring."[32]

The second and third bombings occurred on October 16 and 31; both caused minor leaks in the pipe.[33] All three blasts (and a fourth that occurred in 2009) are believed to be linked.[34]

The pipes that were bombed carry a type of natural gas that "contains deadly hydrogen sulphide, the compound that makes the

---

29. Linda Nguyen & Laura Drake, "$500,000 for B.C. Pipeline Bomb Info," *Canwest News Service*, Jan. 14, 2008.
30. Tiffany Crawford, "Photos of 8 People Released in Pipeline Bombing Case," *Vancouver Sun* (Canada), Dec. 3, 2008
31. Arthur Bright, "Bombings of Canadian Pipelines Spark Ecoterrorism Fears," *Christian Science Monitor*, Oct. 18, 2008.
32. Statement of Mike McAllister, EnCana Vice President of Peace Country Business Unit, Royal Canadian Mounted Police web site, accessed May 26, 2009.
33. Nguyen & Drake, "$500,000 for B.C. Pipeline Bomb Info."
34. "Pipeline Bombings Increasingly Violent: RCMP," *Toronto Star*, Jan. 6, 2009.

gas 'sour.'"[35] Many area residents and activists "believe sour-gas wells pose a risk to the health of humans and livestock."[36]

John Thompson, president of the Toronto-based Mackenzie Institute, commented after the attacks: "This sort of thing has happened before and will happen again. It's almost like the price of doing business... The oil and gas industry is [accustomed] to 'ecotage' and sabotage of various kinds."[37]

Arrest in 1981 Paris Bombing

Nearly thirty years after the bombing of a synagogue in Paris, Lebanese-Canadian citizen Hassan Diab was arrested in Canada. At the time of his arrest, Diab was teaching sociology at the University of Ottawa and Carleton University.

French authorities claimed that Diab made and planted a bomb "that killed four people and injured 20 others on Oct. 3, 1980, outside the Copernic Street synagogue in Paris."[38] France alleged that this is not the only synagogue bombing in which Diab was involved. They also fingered him for responsibility in the October 20, 1981, bombing of a synagogue in Antwerp, Belgium.[39] When the French file on Diab was opened by the order of a Canadian judge, it consisted of four major points:

- Mr. Diab resembles police sketches of the bomber;

- His handwriting matches that of the bomber;

- He is identified by intelligence sources and former friends as having been a member of the Popular Front for the Liberation of Palestine;

- His passport was used to get into France around the time of the 1980 bombing, in suspicious circumstances.[40]

French authorities sought Diab's extradition; under Canadian

35. Laura Drake, "Fear and Loathing Over B.C. Pipeline Blasts," *Canwest News Service*, Jan. 10, 2009.
36. Crawford, "Photos of 8 People Released in Pipeline Bombing Case."
37. Tim Lai, "Sabotage Spreads in the Oilpatch," *Vancouver Sun* (Canada), Oct. 17, 2008.
38. "Ottawa Judge Orders Publication Ban in 1980 Paris Bombing Case," *CBC News* (Canada), Nov. 14, 2008.
39. Kristin Endemann, "Hassan Diab: The French Connection," *Ottawa Citizen*, Nov. 21, 2008.
40. Ibid.

law they were given 45 days to provide legal details for the request.[41] Diab was denied bail in December 2008, pending a decision on his extradition, on the grounds that he may pose a flight risk.[42]

DENMARK

With a relatively small population of 5.4 million, Denmark was not traditionally considered a target for religious terrorism. This changed in September 2005, when the newspaper *Jyllands-Posten* published twelve cartoons caricaturing the Prophet Muhammad, an act prohibited under Islam. Though the response to the cartoons' publication was initially muted, the following year there were outraged reactions—including violence—in a number of Muslim communities around the world. In all, more than 100 people were killed in protests (a large number of these in riots that erupted in Nigeria); Christians living in the Islamic world were targeted; the cartoonists and culture editor of *Jyllands-Posten* received death threats; Western embassies and consulates were attacked in Iran, Lebanon, Libya, and Syria; and a number of symbols of the West (including a Pizza Hut, a Holiday Inn, Western-owned gas stations, and a statue of Ronald McDonald) were attacked by rioters.

Responding to criticism of his decision to publish the cartoons in a February 2006 *Washington Post* op-ed, *Jyllands-Posten* culture editor Flemming Rose insisted that the decision was not a malicious assault on Islam, but was a "response to several incidents of self-censorship in Europe caused by widening fears and feelings of intimidation in dealing with issues related to Islam."[43]

The cartoon controversy reemerged in 2008, when *Jyllands-Posten* republished the contentious images. While public outcry was less hostile than in 2005/06, sites around the world affiliated with Denmark again became potential targets for attack. On June 2, 2008, a car bomb detonated outside the Danish embassy in Pakistan, killing at least six.[44] The attack came less than two months after al-Qaeda's

---

41. In January 2009, Canada's minister of justice gave "the green light for federal prosecutors to move forward with an extradition hearing." Terri Saunders, "Extradition Hearing a Go for Professor," *Ottawa Sun*, Jan. 16, 2009.
42. "Alleged Bomber To Remain In Custody," *National Post* (Canada), Dec. 4, 2008.
43. Flemming Rose, "Why I Published Those Cartoons," *Washington Post*, Feb. 19, 2006.
44. Omar Waraich & Andrew Buncombe, "Danish Embassy Bombed in Protest at Cartoons," *Independent* (London), June 3, 2008.

second-in-command Ayman al-Zawahiri called for attacks on Danish targets: "I admonish and incite every Muslim who is able to do so to cause damage to Denmark in order to show your support for our Prophet, may Allah bless him and grant him salvation, and to defend his esteemed honour."[45] A statement posted on June 5, 2008, by an al-Qaeda commander based in Afghanistan claimed responsibility for the embassy attack, and "threatened more attacks on countries where cartoons of the Prophet Muhammad are published."[46]

The major likely terrorist incident of 2008 that occurred within Denmark's borders came on the last day of the year, when a Lebanese-born Palestinian Danish citizen shot two Israelis at the Rosengaard Mall in Odense. Neither of the men shot were seriously injured; one was shot in the leg, and the other in the hand.[47] The shooter surrendered to police the following day.

The reason this is considered a likely terrorist incident (that is, with underlying political motivations) is because of the backdrop of Israel's incursion into the Gaza Strip from December 2008 to January 2009. The shooting occurred on the fifth day of the conflict, in which Israel invaded Gaza in an effort to stop the smuggling of arms to Hamas. The human cost of this conflict, as well as the devastation of Gaza's infrastructure—broadcast throughout the globe—generated widespread expressions of outrage. These circumstances led many in the Danish media to conclude that the shooting was related to ongoing events in the Middle East.[48]

The suspect's name was not immediately released due to the ongoing nature of the investigation.

FINLAND

Finland has remained on the periphery of the terrorist threat. In a 2004 report, Toby Archer, a researcher at the Finnish Institute of International Affairs, notes, "[t]he dangers of terrorism for Finland

---

45. Quoted in Qandeel Siddique, "Danish Embassy Bombing in Islamabad and Pakistan's Security Situation," Forsvarets Forskningsinstitutt, June 11, 2008.
46. Matthew Pennington, "Al-Qaida Claims Danish Embassy Attack in Pakistan," *Associated Press*, June 5, 2008.
47. "Suspect Surrenders in Danish Mall Shooting," *CNN Wire*, Jan. 1, 2009.
48. See "Danish Police Arrest Palestinian on Suspicion of Shooting Israelis at Shopping Mall," *Reuters*, Jan. 2, 2009.

are, on a global scale, *very low.*[49] Archer states that for a terrorist to attack, he must "have the ability to carry out an attack" as well as "the motivation." In Finland's case, both are lacking. The country's ethnic homogeneity makes it difficult for terrorists of non-Finnish ethnic origin (such as many Islamic militants) to blend in, and there are also "many good reasons to doubt whether non-domestically based terrorists would have much motivation to attack Finland or Finnish targets."[50] However, the country's net migration rate has steadily increased since 2002.

The incident in 2008 that is most likely to be classified as terrorism involved members of Finland's Kurdish population. On October 21, an arson attack occurred at the Turkish embassy in Helsinki,[51] injuring one embassy employee. However, firefighters were able to quickly extinguish the fire.

The early-morning attack occurred hours after Kurdish protestors staged a peaceful anti-Turkey demonstration that coincided with Kurdish demonstrations in Turkey reacting to allegations that Kurdish Workers Party (PKK) leader Abdullah Ocalan was suffering abuse in Turkish custody. (Ocalan, a longtime PKK leader, had been arrested by Turkey in 1999.) A Molotov cocktail attack against the Turkish consulate in Salzburg, Austria, two days earlier led Turkey's ambassador to Finland to claim that the two attacks were both "connected" and "politically motivated." Indeed, a Finnish police spokesman later revealed that some of the young men arrested for the arson were of Kurdish background.

There would be guilty pleas in this case in 2009, coupled with the admission of a political motivation for the attack:

> Three people charged with setting fire to the Turkish embassy in Helsinki October last year told the Helsinki district court on Thursday they had planned the arson in a pub over drinks hours before the attack. One of the youths admitted he had been drunk at the time of the attack and added he had been angered by news of the assault of a Kurd leader in Turkey. The defendant, who

---

49. Toby Archer, *International Terrorism and Finland* (Helsinki: Finnish Institute for International Affairs, 2004), p. 10.
50. Ibid.
51. See "Arson Attack on Turkish Embassy in Finland," *USA Today*, Oct. 21, 2008.

had taken part in a demonstration against the Turkish government the day of the arson attack, added that the trio had persuaded a driver and a fifth individual to join them before procuring some rags and petrol for Molotov's cocktails and driving to the embassy. All five were read arson charges, with Leena Metsäpelto, a state prosecutor, saying the attack had been politically motivated.[52]

Though the perpetrators of this act were angered by the alleged mistreatment of a PKK leader, there were no allegations of a PKK role in the arson. However, as the discussion of the PKK at the end of this section shows, the PKK has been quite active in Europe.

FRANCE

France has had troubles integrating immigrants, particularly those of North African origin. This has contributed to the country's terrorist threat. While there are no official statistics on religious affiliations in France, credible estimates hold that about four to five million Muslims live there, corresponding to around 7-8% of the population. The majority of France's Muslims are originally from the former French colonies of North Africa. In recent years, the world has watched the French suburbs (*banlieues*) erupt in violence. While many of the rioters were Muslim, "the unrest was not about religion. It was not even really about politics; it was about the social and living conditions of the young and of course, about discrimination."[53]

Terrorism remains a threat to France, particularly from Algerian networks.

Multiple Arrests in Three Countries

In May 2008, a three-country police sweep of individuals suspected of terrorist financing resulted in ten arrests in France, Germany, and the Netherlands.[54] Though the individuals' names and nationalities were not released, "officials said they were Turkic-

---

52. "Helsinki Turkish Embassy Arson Planned Over Pints," *STT*, Mar. 12, 2009.
53. Justin Vaisse, "Unrest in France, November 2005: Immigration, Islam and the Challenge of Integration," The Brookings Institution, Jan. 10, 2006, p. 3.
54. John Leicester, "10 Arrested in France, Germany, Netherlands in Terror Probe," *Associated Press*, May 17, 2008.

speaking." The suspects were believed to have collected funds for the Islamic Movement of Uzbekistan (IMU), but they may also have been raising money for a Turkish jihadist group. Specifically, the Dutch National Prosecutor's office alleged that "the suspect arrested in the Netherlands is thought to have received funds collected for a movement led by Metin Kaplan, an Islamic militant accused of attempting to overthrow Turkey's secular regime." Louis Caprioli, former head of counterterrorism at France's DST (Direction de la Surveillance du Territoire), told the press that financial links between Uzbek and Turkish groups may be due to shared goals, as well as ethnic and linguistic commonalities.[55]

Eight of the arrests took place in France. The individual arrested in Germany was apprehended at France's request.[56] Though he lived in France, he was staying in Weil am Rhein in Germany's Baden-Württemberg state at the time of the arrests. The tenth man held was captured in Tilburg, in the Netherlands.

Paris Store Targeted

In December 2008, explosives were found in the Printemps Haussmann department store in Paris.[57] A previously unknown group calling itself the Afghan Revolutionary Front sent a letter to the French news agency AFP warning that "several bombs" were in the store, and stating: "Send the message to your president that he must withdraw his troops from our country before the end of February 2009 or else we will take action in your capitalist department stores and this time, without warning."[58] The explosives were described by officials as "five sticks of dynamite bound together with a cord in a restroom on the third floor of the men's store."[59] No detonator was found with them, leading French officials to conclude that there was no intent to set off an explosion.

---

55. Ibid.
56. Yassin Musharbash, "Police Arrest Members of Alleged Jihadi Financing Network," *Spiegel Online* (Germany), May 16, 2008.
57. "Explosives Found in Paris Store," *BBC News*, Dec. 16, 2008.
58. Ibid. A thorough search using both the French and English translation of the group's name reveals that the only time it has been referenced is in relation to this incident. The "Afghan Revolutionary Front" has not claimed responsibility for any other attacks.
59. Katrin Bennhold & Basil Katz, "Explosives Found at Paris Department Store," *New York Times*, Dec. 16, 2008.

GERMANY

Germany's immigration issues have contributed to cleavages within the country, as it hosts Europe's largest immigrant population. Germany has about 15 million immigrants, comprising almost 20% of the population.[60] Examining the origins of Germany's immigrant population, the former Soviet states rank first, with ethnic Turks comprising the second largest migrant group (approximately 3 million). The Berlin Institute for Population and Development has found that immigrants' country of origin correlated to their success integrating into German society, with Turkish immigrants "the most poorly integrated group in Germany." Parallel societies have emerged in some of Germany's ethnic communities.

Non-German unemployment rates are twice as high as the national average, and a 2008 Pew Global Attitudes Project poll found that 50% of Germans held an unfavorable opinion of Muslims.[61] Of Germany's 3 million Muslims, approximately 100,000 are converts to the faith.

Germany's First Suicide Bomber Strikes[62]

Cüneyt Ciftci's last mission began on a Monday afternoon at 4.30 p.m. On March 3, 2008, the 28-year-old German-raised Turk from Ansbach in Bavaria drove a blue Toyota pickup truck in front of a military building used by NATO in Afghanistan's Khost province and pushed a button. Hundreds of kilograms of explosives blew up, causing part of the building to collapse. Two U.S. soldiers, two civilians, and Ciftci himself died. This act made him Germany's first suicide bomber.[63]

Ciftci's story represents a recent development in the homegrown terrorist threat that Germany faces. According to the Federal Criminal Police Office (*Bundeskriminalamt*), more than 50 young men residing in Germany visited terror training camps in Pakistan during 2008. It is striking to note the high number of converts among those radicals,

---

60. Germany's demographic figures are taken from the Berlin Institute for Population and Development.
61. *Unfavorable Views of Jews and Muslims on the Increase in Europe* (Washington, D.C.: Pew Global Attitudes Project, Sept. 17, 2008), p. 16.
62. We would like to gratefully acknowledge the assistance of *Stern Magazine* in Hamburg, Germany, which provided a great deal of information about Cüneyt Ciftci.
63. Roger Boyes, "Bavarian Cueneyt Ciftci is Germany's First Suicide Bomber," *Times* (London), Mar. 18, 2008.

as well as the high number of second-generation immigrants who were born and raised in Germany.

Ciftci was known as a radical by German authorities for quite some time before his attack, but he was not considered extremely dangerous. He had contact with the Islamic Community of Millis Goerues (Islamische Gemeinschaft Millis Görüs), and with the Tablighi Jamaat, a socially conservative grassroots religious movement with roots in the Indian subcontinent. The Ciftcis were known as a strict religious family.

Cüneyt Ciftci was at a boarding school in Turkey for three years before he returned to Germany, where he had problems in school. Without graduating, and after several short-term jobs, he finally landed a position at the electrical company Bosch in Ansbach. In 2001 he married his wife Seda, whom he met in a doner kebab takeout, and with whom he had two sons. Seda, who grew up in a secular and modern Turkish family, became strictly religious shortly after the marriage.

In March 2007, Cüneyt Ciftci, Seda, and their two children traveled to Pakistan. The trip was organized by a fellow Muslim, Adem Yilmaz from Langen in Hesse (Germany). Yilmaz is believed responsible for having sent at least seven young men to terror training camps in Pakistan. He is a member of the so-called "Sauerland cell," which centered on German convert Fritz Gelowicz. The group is held responsible for planning what would have been Germany's largest terrorist attack. The plot was fortunately disrupted before it could be executed: in September 2007, the plotters were apprehended by German Federal Police special forces, who found them as they were heating a hydrogen peroxide solution in order to concentrate the chemical. According to investigations, the Sauerland cell was affiliated with the terrorist organization Islamic Jihad Union (IJU), an offshoot of the Islamic Movement of Uzbekistan (IMU).

Seda Hendem-Ciftci told the police the details about their trip to Mir Ali near the Afghan border, where they lived in a shack. Her husband took part in military training which was supposedly run by Suhail Buranow, an IJU leader. After two weeks Cüneyt Ciftci announced that he would go on a jihad, and disappeared for weeks. Even though his third child was born in the camp, he felt much closer to his comrades-in-arms than he did to his wife and children.

In December 2007, Seda Hendem-Ciftci and the three children

returned to Germany. Three months later, Cüneyt Ciftci blew himself up. In a videotaped message recorded before his "martyrdom" operation, one can see Ciftci laughing, holding a pistol in his left hand and talking to the audience: "My aim is that my message—God willing—reaches young holy warriors in Turkey and Europe, who carry the love and fire of the jihad in their hearts, and who go on jihad on their way to Allah with heart, soul, goods and chattels. By this suicide attack I'd like to motivate them to do the same."

The Islamic Jihad Union claimed credit for Ciftci's attack. Their statement on the attack said: "He was a brave Turk who came from Germany and exchanged his life of luxury for paradise."

Islamic Jihad Union Showcases its German Member

The Islamic Jihad Union released propaganda videos in 2008 depicting German national Eric Breininger participating in jihad in Afghanistan. Originally from Saarland in western Germany, Breininger converted to Islam in 2007 when he was working for the parcel service and "met a colleague of Pakistani descent who wore a long beard and was enthusiastic about Islam. Breininger was delighted. He embraced the new religion and tossed his cross necklace into a river."[64] Breininger radicalized quickly, with one investigator commenting that he was "a very impressionable person who could have just as easily ended up with the neo-Nazis or Scientology, if he had fallen under their influence."[65]

The videos featuring Breininger promoted jihadist themes. Two videos surfaced in April and May, and another video was released in October. In the October video, Breininger denied reports that he was heading to Germany to carry out an attack, but said that the Germans would be under the threat of terrorism as long as they had troops in Afghanistan and Uzbekistan: "If you withdraw your soldiers from this war which the Americans have begun cautiously, then the Germans will not be targets of the Islamists."[66] He said that the Islamists would "wage war against these occupying powers until we conquer back our countries," and declared "war upon every country that is fighting on the side of America against Muslims."[67]

---

64. Andrea Brandt et al., "From the Rhine River to the Jihad," *Der Spiegel* (Germany), Sept. 29, 2008.
65. Ibid.
66. "Islamic Jihad Union: Eric Breininger Statement," NEFA Foundation, Oct. 21, 2008.
67. Ibid.

Alleged Somali Terrorists Arrested Aboard KLM Flight

Two men in their mid-twenties were arrested and escorted off a KLM flight by German police at the Cologne-Bonn airport in September 2008.[68] The suspects—named in the press as "Abdirazak B." and "Omar D."—were Germans of Somali descent.

According to police spokesman Frank Scheulen, the two men had been under surveillance for months due to "suspicion of participating in a jihad [holy war] action and of possibly planning attacks."[69] Police found documents, including a suicide note, that seemed to confirm the suspects' intent.[70] While investigators believe that the men "were ready to fight and die in a jihad,"[71] an attack was not felt to be imminent, and they did not have weapons on their persons or in their luggage. Rather, authorities believe that the suspects were traveling to Africa. Once there, they may have planned to undertake militant training, participate in the armed struggle in Uganda,[72] or perhaps move on to Pakistan.[73]

Islamic Jihad Union Supporters Arrested

Police in Germany arrested Omid Shirkhani and Huseyin Ozgun in September.[74] They were accused of being linked to a 2007 bomb plot involving converts Fritz Gelowicz and Daniel Martin Schneider. Prosecutors said that Shirkhani "had visited a training camp near the Afghan-Pakistani border run by the terrorist group Islamic Jihad Union," and that Ozgun had provided support to the group.[75] Both men were accused of procuring equipment for the IJU, including night-vision goggles and a GPS device sent to a group member in Iran.[76]

---

68. Brandt et al., "From the Rhine River to the Jihad."

69. "Terror Suspects Held on KLM Plane," *BBC News*, Sept. 26, 2008.

70. Michael Levitin, "Suspected Terrorists Arrested on KLM Plane in Germany," *Telegraph* (London), Sept. 26, 2008.

71. Annika Joeres, "Spektakuläre Festnahme: Zugriff vor Abflug," *Frankfurter Rundschau* (Germany), Sept. 26, 2008.

72. "Staatsanwälte Ermitteln Gegen Mutmaßliche Islamisten," *Der Spiegel* (Germany), Sept. 26, 2008.

73. Brandt et al., "From the Rhine River to the Jihad."

74. Nicholas Kulish, "Germany: 2 Arrested In Bombing Plot," *New York Times*, Sept. 20, 2009.

75. Ibid. Article 129a of the German Criminal Code prohibits support and recruitment for terrorist organizations, as well as terrorist financing.

76. "Two Men Charged with Terrorism in Germany," *Deutsche Welle* (Germany), Mar. 18, 2009.

Two Arrested for Running Jihadist Web Site

On November 25, German police arrested and charged two men for operating a jihadist Web site.[77] The site "contained videos from al-Qaeda, Mesopotamian al-Qaeda and the radical group Ansar al-Islam." Both suspects were German nationals.

Asked how managing a Web site could be considered terrorism, the prosecutors stated: "The operators of GIMF [Global Islamic Media Front] assist the purpose of Islamist terrorist groups to reach the largest possible audience with propaganda that serves to mobilize more supporters and intimidate the western public."[78]

GREECE

Most of the politically-motivated violence that has occurred in Greece in recent years has been perpetrated by nationalist or anarchist groups. One of the nation's most notorious terrorist groups, November 17, seems to have been rendered inactive by the arrest and conviction of fifteen members in 2002/03.[79] The group had been active since the 1970s. Similarly, the leftist terror group Revolutionary People's Struggle (ELA) "disbanded in 1995."[80] More recently, a new group appeared called Revolutionary Struggle (Epanastratikos Aghonas), which is similarly opposed to capitalism and the West. That group emerged in 2003, when it claimed responsibility for a bombing attack on the Athens courthouse complex.[81] Revolutionary Struggle may have a number of members from previous Greek leftist terror groups.

On January 14, 2009, Revolutionary Struggle claimed responsibility for two separate incidents that occured during 2008.[82] In the first incident, a bomb placed outside Royal Dutch Shell's offices in October was defused by police before it caused any damage.[83] Investigators had already linked that incident to Revolutionary Struggle based on the materials used. In the second incident, a police

---

77. "German Police Arrest Two in Connection with Islamist Web Site," *Deutsche Welle* (Germany), Nov. 26, 2008.
78. Ibid.
79. "November 17, Revolutionary People's Struggle, Revolutionary Struggle," *CFR Backgrounder*, updated Jan. 12, 2007.
80. Ibid.
81. "Revolutionary Struggle," *START Terrorist Organization Profile*, accessed May 27, 2009.
82. "Greek Militant Group Claims Responsibility for Attacks on Police," *RTT News*, Jan. 14, 2009.
83. "Greek Police Defuse Small Bomb at Shell HQ," *Associated Press*, Oct. 24, 2008.

bus was shot on December 23 in the midst of violent political protests.

IRELAND

Ireland has long had a significant terrorist presence, in large part due to the conflict in Northern Ireland. Though the ferocity of that conflict has been tempered by attempts at reconciliation like the 1988 Belfast Agreement, splinter groups and armed factions have periodically committed violent acts since then. The most deadly attack occurred in August 1998, when a splinter group of the Provisional Irish Republican Army (IRA), the Real IRA, set off a car bomb on Omagh, Northern Ireland that killed 29 people.

Five Arrested for Kidnap Plot

Five suspected members of the Irish National Liberation Army, another splinter group of the IRA, were arrested on February 22 in the counties of Cork, Kerry, and Limerick, by Ireland's national police.[84] The group had been under surveillance since 2007, when police received a tip that they planned to kidnap a businessman and his family from their home in a wealthy district of Cork.

Shell Ireland Targeted

Energy companies like Shell have been targeted by environmental terrorists. Ireland's most significant terrorist incident in 2008 took aim at Shell Ireland: a crudely constructed bomb was left outside its offices to protest a gas pipeline project in Co Mayo, in the western part of the country.[85] The army bomb disposal squad described the device as "viable, home-made, crude and highly-dangerous."[86]

"We've had a lot of attacks in Mayo. There has [been] fencing torn down, there has been arson attacks. We have had guys reversing through the gates," a Shell Ireland spokesman told the press. "This is a sinister development and very serious escalation. This is another notch up and we're extremely worried."[87]

---

84. "Five Accused of Terrorism After Kidnap Plot Arrests," *Times* (London), Feb. 25, 2008.
85. Ronan McGreevy, "Bomb Squad Defuses Device at Shell HQ," *Irish Times,* Sept. 16, 2008.
86. Ibid.
87. Ibid.

ITALY

In the last twenty years, Italy has changed from a country of emigration to one of immigration; the country faces its most significant terrorist threat at present from radical Islamic groups. Most Muslims in Italy arrived within the last ten to twenty years. Italy's Islamic population comes from a diverse array of backgrounds. In the years since 9/11, "Italy has become a platform for al-Qaeda associated terrorist organizations in Europe and Iraq."[88] The events of 2008 illustrate the country's connections to global Islamic terrorism.

North African Men Arrested

Five North African men were arrested in Bologna in August on international terrorism charges.[89] The ringleader was Khalil Jarraya, a Bosnian war veteran, who had allegedly recruited four other men "to take part in suicide attacks in Afghanistan and Iraq."[90] The cell had been investigated for three years, and following the arrests a police spokesman in Bologna explained: "These are people who were radicalised in the West and declared themselves ready to become martyrs for jihad." In addition to the recruitment for jihad, the suspects were accused of sending money "to Bosnian groups with links to terror organisations in Iraq and Afghanistan."[91] It was alleged that some of these funds were illegally obtained, through fraudulent car accident insurance claims.

During searches, authorities found "1000 pages of documents and four CD-ROMs filled with pictures and videos of decapitations, bodies of suicide bombers and their victims," as well as grotesque propaganda and material to be used for training in weapons and explosives.[92]

Self-Taught Jihadists

Two Moroccan immigrants, Rachid Ilhami and Gafir Abdelkader,

---

88. Kathryn Haahr, "Italy: Europe's Emerging Platform for Islamic Extremism," *Terrorism Monitor,* The Jamestown Foundation, May 5, 2005.

89. "Italy: Five Held in Raid on Terror Suspects," *Associated Press*, Aug. 10, 2008.

90. Ibid.

91. "Italy: Jihadist Terror Suspects Deny Accusations Against Them," *Adnkronos International*, Aug. 12, 2008.

92. Paola Cascella & Alessandro Cori, "In Uno Scatolini i Segreti dei Terroristi," *Repubblica* (Italy), Aug. 10, 2008.

were arrested in December on "on suspicion of planning and carrying out an act of international terrorism."[93] Italian officials claimed that "the two were recruiting men and planning attacks against military and civilian targets, including the immigration office of a police station, a barracks for the Carabinieri—or special paramilitary units—and a shopping center," all around Milan.[94] Though no formal charges were brought immediately, Italian law allows authorities to detain suspects for a year without charge.

The two men were self-taught, according to a source familiar with the investigation who spoke to CNN. The source said that the suspects had not trained in terror camps, had no connections to known terrorist groups, and lacked "the knowledge of how to handle explosives."[95] They attempted to use the Internet to make up for these deficiencies. Bruno Megale, chief of Milan's anti-terrorism unit, described the case as "classic do-it-yourself terrorism."[96]

NORWAY AND SWEDEN

The threat of terrorism in Norway is generally considered low, and the "widespread belief among the general public" has been "that Norway was not in danger of attack."[97] Similarly, Sweden has a relatively low terrorist threat. However, the U.S. Department of State has noted that "terrorist organizations [have] exploited Sweden's considerable legal protections of personal freedoms and civil liberties to maintain a presence in the country."[98]

Norway and Sweden are linked not only as Scandinavian countries with fairly low threats from terrorism, but also because the most significant terrorism-related event in both countries in 2008 was a coordinated action between their governments. In late February, Sweden arrested three men of Somali origin on terrorism financing charges. At the same time, Norwegian police arrested three suspects in

---

93. Alessio Vinci, "Italian Police Arrest Suspects for Alleged Terror Plot," *CNN*, Dec. 2, 2008.
94. Ibid.
95. Ibid.
96. Sebastian Rotella & Maria De Cristofaro, "Italian Investigators Dismantle Alleged Terrorist Cell," *Los Angeles Times*, Dec. 3, 2008.
97. U.S. Department of State, *Country Reports on Terrorism 2008* (Apr. 30, 2009).
98. Ibid.

Oslo, who were also originally from Somalia, on similar charges.[99] The men were suspected of funding the Somali extremist group al-Shabaab.

Before these raids, the chief of Norway's police unit PST (*Politiets sikkerhetstjeneste*) had uncharacteristically spoken to the media about problems his country was experiencing with attempted terrorist recruitment:

> The normally secretive Jørn Holme, chief of the PST, has recently been on a press offensive of sorts, claiming in newspaper *Aftenposten* that terrorists have actively tried to recruit young Norwegian Muslims and that money was suspected of being sent out of the country to finance terrorist attacks overseas. Holme also spoke of "older, manipulative Islamic extremists" who were trying to motivate young Muslims into taking part in *jihad* in foreign countries. Holme called the situation "more complex" than earlier, and said it therefore was necessary for PST to warn of the activity and make Norwegians aware of it. "We need to counter this activity in the community," he said. "We rely on the cooperation of all those who have information about what's happening in extremist Islamic circles."[100]

Two of the men arrested in Norway were released two days later. However, they "still face further investigation and possible charges."[101] The third man was released in June under stringent conditions, including the requirement that he regularly report to the police, turn in his passport, and refrain from leaving the country. Norwegian police insisted that their case against him had not weakened.

Sweden, however, ended up dropping charges entirely against the three men arrested there. In September, the prosecutor stated that "he could not prove that the men had intended to send money to terrorist organizations."[102]

---

99. Nina Berglund, "Three Charged with Financing Terrorist Activity," *Aftenposten* (Norway), Feb. 28, 2008.
100. Ibid.
101. "Norway Frees 2 Men Held in Insurgency Finance Case," *Reuters*, Mar. 1, 2008.
102. "Sweden Drops Charges Against 3 Terror Suspects," *Associated Press*, Sept. 12, 2008.

SPAIN

Spain has a lengthy history of dealing with terrorism. Terrorism in Spain has traditionally involved nationalist movements, particularly from the Basque region, but religious terrorism has emerged in recent years as another major threat. The most dramatic example is the train bombings that occurred on March 11, 2004, three days before the country's general elections.

Suicide Plot Uncovered

Fourteen men, all but two born in Pakistan, were arrested in January for allegedly conspiring to undertake suicide bombings against Barcelona's mass transit system. When an indictment against eleven of them was later made public, a CNN report explained:

> The indictment said the group had achieved "operational capacity" at a human level and was "very close to achieving full technical capacity with explosives" with the alleged aim of "committing various terrorist suicide attacks between last January 18 and 20 on public transport in the city of Barcelona.[103]

The judge in this case, Ismael Moreno, explained that the group had already chosen three men to carry out suicide attacks.[104] All three men had traveled to Barcelona from Pakistan, and all of the individuals arrested belonged to the Tablighi Jamaat, a socially conservative grassroots religious movement with roots in the Indian subcontinent.

In undertaking the investigation, the Spanish intelligence services received information from foreign agencies, but also had an informant among the plotters.

Algerian Men Spreading Radical Ideology

Three Algerian men were arrested in the Basque city of Vitoria on February 14 for "promoting radical ideology among the Muslim community."[105] Police suspected that they had been distributing CDs and MP3 files calling for war against the West. The two major distribution

---

103. Al Goodman, "Spanish Judge Indicts 11 on Terror Charges," *CNN,* June 5, 2008.
104. Martin Hodgson, "Raids Foiled Barcelona Bomb Plot, Says Judge," *Guardian* (U.K.), Jan. 24, 2008.
105. Al Goodman, "Spain Arrests Suspected Islamic Extremists," *CNN*, Feb. 14, 2008.

sites were an apartment and a telephone store "where people without fixed [telephones] often go to make calls or use the Internet."[106]

Arrest of Men Wanted on Terrorism Charges in Morocco

In April, Spanish police in Melilla (a small autonomous Spanish city on Morocco's north coast) arrested two men who were wanted in Morocco on terrorism charges.[107] The first, Ali Aarass, was allegedly involved in the 2003 suicide bombings in Casablanca that killed 32 people as well as the bombers. Police also detained Mohammed El Bay, whom they said "was in charge of striking up links with Central European arms dealers on behalf of an Islamic militant group in Morocco."[108] Spain did not intend to try the men, but instead was going to begin proceedings to extradite them to Morocco.[109]

Operación Submarino Arrests

In June, eight Algerian-born men were arrested for allegedly providing financial and logistical support to al-Qaeda in the Islamic Maghreb (AQIM), al-Qaeda's North African affiliate, as well as "recruiting and indoctrinating members."[110] The Spanish-language press reported that the most fervent supporters of their ideology could end up traveling to Iraq to join the insurgency.[111]

The eight suspects were between 27 and 39 years old. Police seized about 7,000 euros in the raids, "and found evidence of money transfers to Algeria, bank books, telephone cards, CDs, videos and 'diverse' documents."[112] It seems that the suspects did not make use of *hawala* networks, which would have allowed them to move money without going through banks.[113] An interior ministry spokesman described the cell as typical for Spain, "devoted to financing, recruitment and sending warriors to conflict zones."[114] Police also held

---

106. Ibid.
107. Ben Harding, "Spain Arrests Man Wanted for Casablanca Bombing," *Reuters*, Apr. 1, 2008.
108. Ibid.
109. "Spain Holds Morocco Bomb Suspect," *BBC News*, Apr. 2, 2008.
110. Elaine Sciolino, "Spain Arrests 8 It Says Aided a Qaeda-Linked Cell," *New York Times*, June 11, 2008.
111. "ICT Global Terrorism Brief: Spanish Arrests - 09.07.2008," International Institute for Counter-Terrorism (Herzliya, Israel), July 9, 2008.
112. Sciolino, "Spain Arrests 8 It Says Aided a Qaeda-Linked Cell."
113. F. Mercado et al., "La Policía Desarticula una Célula de Financiación y Captación 'Yihadista,'" *El País* (Spain), June 11, 2008.
114. Sciolino, "Spain Arrests 8 It Says Aided a Qaeda-Linked Cell."

ten others with possible links to the suspects.

The arrests were part of an ongoing anti-terror investigation known as Operación Submarino.[115]

Algerian Fundraisers Arrested

Accused of fundraising for terror activities, four men of Algerian origin were arrested on July 1.[116] Specifically, they were accused of "funding insurgency movements in Iraq, Pakistan, Algeria and Iran."[117] However, all of the monetary transfers occurred in small amounts, the largest being 2,400 euros; this contributed to the difficulties authorities experienced in tracing all of them. Not only was some of the cell's money going to finance terrorism, but Spanish authorities alleged that the funds had come from illegal enterprises, such as the sale of counterfeit documents and clothing.

Spanish authorities coordinated with the British in making these arrests because of the Algerians' links to "other suspected extremists in Britain."[118]

AQIM Member Arrested

On August 1, Spanish police announced that they had arrested Kamel Salhi, whom they accused of links to AQIM.[119] Police said that they found "dozens of fake Spanish work contracts for north African immigrants," as well as radical literature.[120] Bank documents allegedly linked him to the cell arrested in June as part of Operación Submarino.

In an interview Salhi gave with a Spanish-language publication following his arrest, he proclaimed his innocence. He claimed that authorities only thought the books and CDs uncovered in searches were radical because they misunderstood the notion of jihad. "Jihad is the effort of any Muslim to be a good Muslim," he said. "This interview

---

115. Ibid.
116. "Spanish Police Arrest 4 Suspected Islamic Extremists Accused of Financing Terror Groups," *International Herald Tribune,* July 1, 2008.
117. "Spain: Alleged al-Qaeda-Linked Islamists Arrested," *Adnkronos International*, July 1, 2008.
118. "Spanish Police Arrest 4 Suspected Islamic Extremists Accused of Financing Terror Groups," *International Herald Tribune*.
119. "Spanish Police Arrest al-Qaeda-Linked Suspect," *AFP*, Aug. 1, 2008.
120. Ibid.

we're doing now is jihad because it tells the truth."[121]

Multiple Arrests in Madrid Train Bombings Investigation

Twelve people were arrested in October 2008, in connection with both the 2004 Madrid train bombings and also ongoing terrorist activity. They were accused of "providing cover for five fugitives from the Madrid train bombings," as well as being involved in ongoing terrorist financing and recruitment.[122]

The ETA Challenge

The Euskadi Ta Azkatasuna (ETA), a Basque nationalist terror group, has been responsible for a great deal of Spain's terrorist violence. ETA originally emerged as a student movement opposed to General Franco's military dictatorship, during which time "the Basque language was banned, their distinctive culture suppressed, and intellectuals imprisoned and tortured for their political and cultural beliefs."[123] Though Spain's Basque region now enjoys autonomy—including its own parliament, an independent police force, control over the region's education, and the power to levy taxes—ETA's violent campaign is now focused on "full independence."[124]

In 2008, ETA's campaign included two assassinations, two bomb-related deaths, injuries to hundreds, and millions of euros in property damage. The group is also heavily involved in criminal activities and extortion, demanding a "revolutionary tax" from Spanish businesses.[125] At the same time, the Spanish government has also launched a crackdown on ETA, its activities, and its front groups.

One of the assassinations that ETA was blamed for in 2008 occurred in March, when a small-town Socialist politician, Isaias Carrasco, was shot to death in Mondragon. He "was shot three times in his car as he prepared to go to his job as a clerk in a highway toll booth."[126] Carrasco had served on the town council for four years, and his killing was triggered by the fact that he "was one of just a handful of non-nationalist members in a town where pro-independence

---

121.   Yolanda Tena, "Kamel Salhi: 'Si Fuera Terrorista Hubiese Puesto ya una Bomba,'" *Mediterráneo* (Spain), Aug. 6, 2008.

122.   "Spain Makes Train Bomb-Related Terror Arrests," *CNN*, Oct. 16, 2008.

123.   "Who Are Eta?," *BBC News*, Nov. 17, 2008.

124.   Ibid.

125.   Javier Espinoza, "Spanish Terrorism Boosts Security Sector," *Forbes*, Apr. 28, 2008.

126.   Daniel Woolls, "Spain Mourns on Eve of Election," *Associated Press*, Mar. 8, 2008.

sentiment is fierce."[127] The other assassination attributed to the group was the murder of businessman Ignacio Uría, 70, whose construction firm Altuna y Uría had been building part of the high-speed rail line connecting Spain's Basque region to Madrid and France. ETA had "threatened many companies and their workers involved in the train project as it views such construction as an imposition on the Basque Country by the Spanish and French governments."[128] Uría himself had received a number of threats directly from ETA.

One of the car bombings attributed to ETA in 2008 occurred in the Basque village of Legutiano in May. In that attack, which the Spanish government described as an "attempted massacre," a pre-dawn bombing near a police barracks "blew off part of the building's roof, raining down debris and trapping people inside."[129] Twenty-nine people lived in the targeted building, including five children; one policeman was killed and four wounded. ETA was also blamed for a series of blasts in September that struck Vitoria, Ondarroa, and Cantabria. The targets were a regional bank's headquarters, a police station, and a military academy. The third of these bombings killed a 46-year-old Spanish army sergeant who was on holiday with his wife, and injured six people.[130]

There were a large number of other incidents related to ETA's offensive. Some of these include:

> *February 8*: ETA's first attack in 2008 employed a rucksack bomb, targeting the Bergara court building. The bomb went off shortly after midnight, 24 minutes after an anonymous caller warned authorities about the impending attack. There was extensive property damage, but no casualties.

> *February 23*: A TV transmitter on the outskirts of Bilbao was damaged by an ETA bomb several hours after authorities received a warning call. The explosive device was estimated at 3-4 kg, and was detonated by police using a robotic device.

---

127. Ibid.
128. Graham Keeley, "Eta Shoots Dead Businessman Working on High-Speed Spanish Train Link," *Times* (London), Dec. 3, 2008.
129. Alberto Letona, "Car Bomb Blamed on Basque Militants Kills Policeman in Spain," *Associated Press*, May 14, 2008.
130. Jane Walker, "Spanish Soldier Killed in Eta Blast," *Irish Times*, Sept. 23, 2008.

February 29: Ten days before Spain's national elections, the Socialist party office in the Basque town of Derio was targeted by an ETA bomb. A warning call in ETA's name was made shortly after midnight, and the explosion occurred around 1:00 a.m. The office was damaged, but nobody was injured.[131]

March 21: A car bomb exploded outside a Calahorra police station following a warning call from ETA. Major property damage resulted from the blast but a successful evacuation meant that only one person was hurt, as a police officer received a slight neck injury.[132]

March 30: Two small bombs exploded at a radio repeater station in Guipúzcoa province, causing minor damage but no injuries. Although ETA phoned in a warning, weather conditions prevented security forces from accessing and defusing the bombs in time.

April 12: ETA planted two bombs near telecommunications transmitters in Navarre. One of the devices, which exploded around 11:00 a.m., was intended as a booby trap for security forces.

April 17: A bomb blast "injured seven police and caused major damage to the offices of Spain's ruling Socialist party" in Bilbao.[133] A warning was phoned in prior to the explosion.

April 20: A blast similar to the April 17 attack targeted the Socialist party offices in Elgoibar. No one was injured, as police received a warning call with enough time for a complete evacuation.[134]

May 1: ETA set off three bombs in two locations in the Basque region, damaging an industrial pavilion for vehicles from Spain's ministry of labor and a regional government labor institute. Nobody was injured.[135]

131. Al Goodman, "Bomb Blast in Spain Ahead of Elections," *CNN*, Feb. 29, 2008.
132. Harold Heckle, "Eta Continues Campaign of Violence with Car-Bomb Attack at Police HQ," *Independent* (London), Mar. 22, 2008.
133. "Suspected ETA Blast Injures 7 Spanish Police," *AFP*, Apr. 17, 2008.
134. "ETA Bomb Damages Spanish Ruling Party's Office," *VOA News*, Apr. 20, 2008.
135. Al Goodman, "ETA Blamed for Trio of Bomb Blasts," *CNN*, May 1, 2008.

May 19: ETA detonated a car bomb that damaged a yacht club in Getxo as the head of the Basque regional government was to visit Madrid to improve political relations. The explosion "tore a hole in the ground and could be heard" for several miles, but did not cause any injuries.[136]

May/June:Construcciones Amenábar, a company involved in building a high-speed train linking Spanish cities, was targeted by ETA bombs in Zarautz and Hermnani, both in northern Spain. There were three minor injuries.[137]

September 16: A limpet mine attached to a policeman's private car failed to explode in Bilbao because the motion sensor that should have triggered it failed. Earlier in the day, another dud explosive was found at the home of a different regional police officer.

October 30: A car bomb exploded on the University of Navarra campus in the north of Spain following an ETA warning. Along with severe property damage, seventeen people were injured by flying glass. The explosion occurred around 10:00 a.m. two days after the arrests of three ETA members in Navarra.[138]

ETA's 2008 offensive also manifested itself in numerous other incidents, including the targeting of seaside resorts, highway construction sites, court buildings, a train station, a university campus, a television station, and a Spanish newspaper.

Along with ETA's offensive, Spain tried to crack down on the terrorist group in 2008. Soeren Kern, a senior fellow for transatlantic relations at Madrid's Grupo de Estudios Estratégicos (Strategic Studies Group), explains:

> If ETA has been active during 2008, so have the Spanish authorities. After ETA answered the Zapatero government's eagerness to negotiate by bombing the Madrid airport in December 2006, the Socialist

---

136. "ETA Sets Off Car Bomb on Eve of Spain-Basque Leaders' Talks," *AFP*, May 19, 2008.
137. Harold Heckle, "3 Injured in Bombing in Spain's Basque Country," *Associated Press*, June 1, 2008.
138. Daniel Woolls, "Bomb at University in Spain's Pamplona Wounds 17," Associated Press, Oct. 30, 2008.

government did an about-face and has taken a hard-line approach against the terrorist group ever since. Spain has also improved its counter-terrorism cooperation with neighboring France, a rear-guard logistics base where ETA operatives have traditionally sought safe-haven. Spanish authorities, ranging from the Socialist government to the courts and to the police, have worked to choke off support for ETA, with many arrests of ETA suspects, convictions at trial, restrictions on political activities of known ETA supporters and a crackdown on clandestine ETA financing.[139]

UNITED KINGDOM

The U.K. has a long history of coping with terrorism and political violence. In the past, the predominant group striking at British targets was the Irish Republican Army (IRA). Now, however, British authorities are more focused on the challenge of Islamic terrorism. Some of the largest terrorist attacks and foiled plots since 9/11 have taken place in the U.K. Attempting to put the magnitude of the problem into context, then-MI5 director general Dame Eliza Manningham-Buller said in a rare public speech in late 2006:

> What I can say is that today, my officers and the police are working to contend with some 200 groupings or networks, totalling over 1600 identified individuals (and there will be many we don't know) who are actively engaged in plotting, or facilitating, terrorist acts here and overseas. The extremists are motivated by a sense of grievance and injustice driven by their interpretation of the history between the West and the Muslim world. This view is shared, in some degree, by a far wider constituency. If the opinion polls conducted in the UK since July 2005 are only broadly accurate, over 100,000 of our citizens consider that the July 2005 attacks in London were justified.... We are aware of numerous plots to kill people and to damage our economy. What do I mean by numerous? Five? Ten? No, nearer thirty—

---

139. Soeren Kern, "Spain Cracks Down on ETA ... and ETA Fights Back," GEES Strategic Studies Group, Nov. 3, 2008.

that we know of. These plots often have links back to Al-Qaida in Pakistan and through those links Al-Qaida gives guidance and training to its largely British foot soldiers here on an extensive and growing scale.[140]

Beyond religiously-inspired terrorism, the United Kingdom has also experienced right-wing and environmental terrorism.

Couple Arrested for Publishing Terrorist Material

A married couple, Amjad Mahmood and Shella Roma, was arrested on February 3 and charged with distributing terrorist propaganda.[141] They allegedly designed and printed 200 leaflets calling for Muslims to fight a jihad, and Mahmood "is also said to have distributed leaflets outside his local mosque."[142]

The prosecutor said of the material that the couple produced: "The document contains encouragement to others to go and fight abroad and discusses the issue of Jihad and that war has been declared on Muslims. The two defendants entered into a joint enterprise. The document was well thought-out, carefully planned, articulately written, and some research has gone into it."[143] The prosecutor also revealed that British authorities launched an investigation after the couple went to Colour Copy Express to make photocopies of the pamphlet. One of the employees, a former police officer, "had a look at it and was concerned by what he saw. He gave the documents to the defendants and took the original to the police station and made a report."[144]

The couple was charged under Section 2 of the Terrorism Act of 2006, which provides criminal penalties for an individual who, among other things, "distributes or circulates a terrorist publication," or "gives, sells or lends such a publication."[145] Roma, who authored the pamphlet, received a three-year community order with a two-year supervision requirement after pleading guilty.[146]

---

140. Dame Eliza Manningham-Buller, "The International Terrorist Threat to the U.K.," Speech at Queen Mary's College, London, Nov. 9, 2006.
141. "Terror Pamphlet Charge Two Bailed," *BBC News*, Feb. 12, 2008.
142. "Bail for Couple Accused of Pro-Terrorism Propaganda," *Oldham Advertiser* (U.K.), Feb. 13, 2008.
143. Ibid.
144. Ibid.
145. Terrorism Act of 2006, § 2.2(a), (b) (U.K.).
146. "'Holy War' Mum Spared Jail," *Manchester Evening News* (U.K.), Mar. 30, 2009.

Muslim Teenager Found with Explosives

On April 17, Andrew Ibrahim, age 19, was arrested and held by Avon and Somerset Police.[147] A "suspicious substance" was found in his home, resulting in police carrying out a controlled detonation just after the arrest, with two more detonations following on Saturday. Following an observed pattern in homegrown "jihadi" terrorists, there was a noticeable uptick in Ibrahim's religiosity prior to the incident. The *Times* of London reports:

> A teenage terror suspect was a spiky-haired and pierced techno music fan before he changed his image, dressed in robes and grew a beard.... A picture of Ibrahim on the social networking website MySpace shows him with dyed red hair and facial piercings. His profile also lists his favourite music as hardcore, trance and techno. He describes himself as a non-smoking teetotal Muslim, but has not visited his page since 2006. A source, who says he worked with the teenager said Ibrahim's appearance has changed dramatically since the picture was taken.... The source said he had endured a "difficult few years" and had been "unsettled". "He was struggling in life but I had no idea he had become a Muslim before I saw him two weeks ago," the man said. "I could not believe my eyes. He was dressed in full robes and had a beard. He must have undergone a massive change in identity."[148]

At the end of April, Ibrahim was charged with intending to commit acts of terrorism, possession of explosives, and possession of articles for terrorist purposes.[149] These materials "included a CD Rom, two home-made vests, a quantity of ball bearings, a quantity of air gun pellets, a quantity of nails and screws, wired circuitry, batteries and electric bulb filaments."[150] The explosive substance he possessed was reportedly hexamethylene triperoxide diamine (HMTD).[151] Avon and Somerset Police Assistant Chief Constable Jackie Roberts commented,

---

147. Dominic Tobin, "Suspicious Substance Detonated at Bristol Home," *Times* (London), Apr. 19, 2008.

148. Ibid. For further discussion of homegrown jihadi terrorists and patterns of religiosity, see Daveed Gartenstein-Ross & Laura Grossman, *Homegrown Terrorists in the U.S. and U.K.: An Empirical Examination of the Radicalization Process* (Washington, D.C.: FDD Press, 2009).

149. "Teenager Terror Suspect Charged," *Independent* (U.K.), Apr. 29, 2008.

150. Ibid.

151. Nico Hines, "Bristol Teen Remanded on Terror Charges," *Times* (London), Apr. 30, 2008.

"From our initial inquiries, we are satisfied that he was working alone."[152]

On June 16, a second teenager, Hashi Ahmed Omer, was arrested in Bristol and charged with failing to disclose information that he knew about Ibrahim's plot.

Two Charged With Planning a Terrorist Attack

Two men, Mohammed Abushamma and Qasim Abukar, were arrested on terrorism charges in late April. The men were arrested when they got off a flight at Heathrow Airport on suspicion that they were planning terrorist attacks abroad.[153] Both men were from North London.

In November, Abushamma pled guilty to attempting to reach Afghanistan with the intention of joining mujahidin who were fighting coalition forces. Abukar pled not guilty, and is awaiting trial.[154]

Nicky Reilly's Homemade Bomb

On May 22, 2008, 22-year-old British convert Nicky Reilly—who suffered from mental disabilities—attempted to set off a rudimentary homemade nail bomb in the Giraffe restaurant in Exeter. However, the device failed to work properly: it detonated in Nicky's hands in the restroom, injuring no one but himself.

Plymouth resident Reilly had converted to Islam around the age of seventeen. For a time, he regularly attended local mosques. However, local religious leaders noted that he had not been seen for around six months before the attack, as he seemed to prefer "the company of a smaller group of Muslim men whom he would meet at a local fish-and-chip shop and a halal fast-food shack."[155]

Reilly was frequently described as a "gentle giant," with the mental capacity of a child. The British press noted that he was "believed to have Asperger's syndrome, a form of autism, and may also suffer

---

152. "Teenager Terror Suspect Charged."
153. "British Police Arrest 2 Men Suspected of Planning Terrorist Attacks Overseas," *Associated Press*, Apr. 22, 2008.
154. "British Muslim, Mohammed Abushamma, Admits Terror Charge," *Times* (London), Nov. 29, 2008.
155. Jamie Doward, "Inside Bizarre World of the Big Friendly Giant," *Observer* (London), May 25, 2008.

from schizophrenia."[156] This diminished mental capacity raised serious concerns about emerging terrorist tactics. Both the MI5 and British police stated that his mental disability "may indicate a new strategy of targeting vulnerable people with mental health problems to carry out attacks."[157]

A suicide note that Reilly left in his bedroom was released in January 2009. In it, Reilly explained his grievances, and insisted that he had not been brainwashed:

> Everywhere Muslims are suffering at the hands of Britain, Israel and America. We are sick of taking all the brutality from you. You have imprisoned over 1,000 Muslims in Britain alone in your war on Islam. You torture and destroy Muslim lives by taking a father or a son or a brother, even you torture Muslim women. In Britain it's OK for a girl to have sex without marriage and if she gets pregnant she can get an abortion so easily. When you are getting drunk on Friday and Saturday night your behaviour is worse than animals. You have sex in nightclub toilets. You urinate in shop doorways. You shout your foul and disgusting mouth off in the street. It is unacceptable to Allah and the true religion Islam. Britain and USA and Israel have no real rules. All us Muslims have seen the pictures of Abu Ghraib prison in Iraq, and you all know what you do to our brothers in Guantanamo Bay. Sheikh Usama has told you the solution on how to end this war between us and many others have as well but you ignore us. Our words are dead until we give them life with our blood. Leave our lands and stop your support for Israel. I have not been brainwashed or indoctrinated. I am not insane. I am not doing it to escape a life of problems or hardships. I am doing what God wants from his mujahideen. We love death as you love life.[158]

In October, Reilly pleaded guilty to attempted murder. At the end of January 2009, he was sentenced to life in prison; he must serve

156. David Leppard & Abul Taher, "MI5 Fears Jihadis Will Use Mentally Ill as Suicide Bombers," *Times* (London), May 25, 2008.
157. Ibid.
158. "Suicide Note Attacks Britons," *This is Exeter* (Exeter, U.K.), Jan. 30, 2009.

a minimum of eighteen years for his crimes.

Three Charged in Publisher Plot

Three men—Ali Beheshti, 40, Abrar Mirza, 22, and Abbas Taj, 30—were arrested late in the year, and charged with conspiring to damage the home and office of the publisher of the controversial novel *The Jewel of Medina*, by American author Sherry Jones.[159] The novel—a historical romance that followed the life of Muhammad's young wife Aisha—"became a cause célèbre when Random House dropped it in August 2008 just before publication, citing fear of threats from Muslims."[160] In its statement announcing the cancellation of *The Jewel of Medina*, Random House claimed: "After sending out advance editions of the novel *The Jewel of Medina*, we received in response, from credible and unrelated sources, cautionary advice not only that the publication of this book might be offensive to some in the Muslim community, but also that it could incite acts of violence by a small, radical segment."[161]

Arrests Made in Investigation of Threats

In August, three men were charged as part of an investigation into an assassination threat made on the Internet against Prime Minister Gordon Brown and former Prime Minister Tony Blair. The BBC noted that "no actual plot was in place but officers discovered a written threat on an extremist jihadi website."[162]

In addition to the Internet threat, Ishaq Kanmi was charged with "belonging or professing to belong to al Qaeda, inviting support for al Qaeda, and dissemination of terrorist publications," while Abbas Iqbal and Ilyas Iqbal were charged with "possession of an article in circumstances which give rise to a reasonable suspicion that possession is for a purpose connected with the commission, preparation or instigation of an act of terrorism."[163]

Two more men were arrested in late August for their role in the threats. Muhammad Ali Mumtaz Ahmad was accused of "having material such as camouflage clothes and plans for 'urban combat,'" and was charged with possessing an article that could be useful

---

159. "Three Charged Over Novel Attack," *BBC News,* Oct. 2, 2008.
160. Robert Spencer, Review of *The Jewel of Medina, Middle East Quarterly*, Winter 2009.
161. Press Release, The Random House Publishing Group, accessed June 18, 2009.
162. "'PM Terror Threat' Three Charged," *BBC News*, Aug. 28, 2008.
163. Ibid.

for preparing for or instigating an act of terrorism.[164] A fifth man implicated in the threats, Krenar Lusha, was charged with five terrorist offenses, including possession of four kilograms of potassium nitrate, and "collecting or recording information likely to be useful to someone wanting to commit or prepare a terrorist act."[165]

Woman Charged with Terrorism Offenses

On October 17, Houria Chahed Chentouf was arrested by the Greater Manchester Police, and was charged with "keeping a computer memory stick for terror-related purposes."[166] She was arrested after the police executed searches in Manchester and the Netherlands. After Chentouf made a court appearance, the judge "said she would remain in custody due to the severity of the charge."[167]

UNITED STATES

The United States has experienced the full range of terrorist activities. While Islamic terrorism has been the government's major preoccupation since 9/11, terrorism events in the U.S. during 2008 encompassed animal rights extremists, ecoterrorism, and narcoterrorist groups.

Houses Torched Outside Seattle

In early March, five luxury homes in a Seattle suburb were torched in an arson attack; three of the homes were destroyed.[168] The Earth Liberation Front (ELF) claimed responsibility for the attack. The fires were caused by explosive devices that investigators found later.[169] While the developer claimed that these homes were eco-friendly, the arsonists left propaganda mocking these claims:

> A white sheet spray-painted in red was found on a nearby fence. It said, "Built Green? Nope black!" and "McMansions in RCDs r not green," a reference to rural cluster developments. The sheet was signed ELF, the

164. "'PM Threat'—Fourth Man Remanded," *BBC News,* Sept. 2, 2008.
165. "Fifth Man Facing Terror Charges," *BBC News,* Sept. 9, 2008.
166. "Woman Remanded on Terror Charge," *BBC News*, Nov. 1, 2008.
167. Ibid.
168. Paul Shukovsky, "Agents Comb Torched Homes for Clues," *Seattle Post-Intelligencer,* Mar. 4, 2008.
169. Andrea Stone, "Eco-Terror Suspected in Seattle Blazes," *USA Today,* Mar. 3, 2008.

initials of the radical Earth Liberation Front.[170]

The homes were being built near the headwaters of a creek inhabited by the endangered Chinook salmon, and near an aquifer that provides drinking water.

According to the FBI, ELF "is responsible for about 100 arsons across 20 states since 1995."[171] The group has neither leaders nor membership lists, and a spokesman for the group once said that the only way to join was committing an offense in its name. As an FBI special agent told the Seattle press, "ELF is an ideology more than a structured organization."[172]

World's Leading Arms Trafficker Arrested

Viktor Bout, the world's leading arms trafficker, was arrested at a Bangkok hotel on March 6 while attempting to buy weapons for the Colombian narcoterrorist group Revolutionary Armed Forces of Colombia (FARC). In May, the U.S. Attorney for the Southern District of New York unsealed an indictment charging Bout with conspiracy to kill U.S. nationals, conspiracy to kill U.S. officers or employees, conspiracy to acquire and use an anti-aircraft missile, and conspiracy to provide material support or resources to a designated foreign terrorist organization based on his activities on FARC's behalf. This is because the U.S. believes that Bout was making the deal for FARC with the understanding that the weapons would be used against American helicopters in Colombia.

Bout had extensive international business interests. He has allegedly been involved in arms deals in Afghanistan, Angola, the Democratic Republic of Congo, Liberia, Rwanda, South America, Sudan, and elsewhere. His client list has included the Taliban, al-Qaeda, Liberian dictator Charles Taylor, and Marxist rebel groups—but also the American and British militaries, and the United Nations.

As 2009 began, Bout was fighting extradition to the United States.

---

170. Ibid.
171. Jonathan Martin & Mike Carter, "Arson Group Retreats Even More into Shadows," *Seattle Times*, Mar. 18, 2008.
172. Stone, "Eco-Terror Suspected in Seattle Blazes."

The Significance of Viktor Bout's Arrest
By Douglas Farah

The March 6, 2008, arrest of Viktor Bout, one of the world's largest private weapons merchants, was a significant blow to the growing nexus of organized crime and terrorism. Bout, whose activities helped fuel wars across Africa, Afghanistan and Latin America, was targeted by the Drug Enforcement Administration (DEA) because he was one of the world's premier "shadow facilitators." The term is used to describe a select group of individuals who are able to service multiple organizations across the political and ideological board, from terrorists to criminals to the United Nations and state militaries. His business activities stood at the crossroads of licit and illicit, the useful and the criminal. His arrest was important because it damaged several organizations simultaneously, and signaled a paradigm shift in identifying and attacking this type of transnational syndicate.

Bout began his career after leaving the Soviet military as an intelligence officer with a noted gift for languages. He quickly found that the marriage of the two commodities to which he had access in the post-Cold War world—weapons and airplanes—could make him and his patrons within the old intelligence structure rich because he could offer door-to-door delivery of valuable commodities. In the emerging free market arms races that included both state and non-state actors, particularly in Sub-Saharan Africa, this service was highly valued.

Among his distinguished rogue and terrorist clients Bout counted Charles Taylor of Liberia, Moammar Gadaffi of Libya, the Taliban in Afghanistan, Jonas Savimbi of the UNITA rebels in Angola, Mobutu Sese Seko of Zaire (now the Democratic Republic of Congo), the Revolutionary Armed Forces of Colombia (FARC), Hizballah, and many others.

At the same time, Bout provided legitimate air fleet services to a host of actors, including the U.S. military in its resupply operations in Iraq, the British military, and the United Nations in its peacekeeping missions and disaster relief efforts. His actions were not dictated by ideology or theology, but by the potential profit involved.

It was that ethos that shaped Bout's growth into the essential supplier of anyone who wanted his products, shifting away from the Cold War paradigm of ideologically-motivated and state controlled weapons supplies to non-state actors.

What made the Bout operation particularly lethal was its ability to greatly improve the quality of weapons being used by non-state actors across the globe, many of whom had stated intentions to inflict damage on the United States. While many traffickers could deliver a few hundred AK-47 assault rifles or a few thousand rounds of ammunition, Bout's ability to deliver complex weapons systems (surface to air missiles, land mines, anti-aircraft guns, attack helicopters, etc.) in a short period of time, to virtually anywhere in the world, made his operation unique. His weapons deliveries greatly enhanced the firepower of groups like the Revolutionary United Front (RUF) in Sierra Leone, whose signature atrocity was the amputation of the arms and legs of men, women, and children, and the systematic use of rape as a control mechanism.

Because of the scope of Bout's clientele and the range of services he provided, from weapons procurement to the acquiring of End User Certificates to transportation, his arrest hurt several parts of different criminal and terrorist organizations. Bout delivered weapons to Hizballah in the summer 2006 war, and had delivered weapons to the militias in Nigeria's Niger Delta in the months before his arrest. He was arrested during a sting operation in which he agreed to sell surface-to-air missiles to people he thought represented the FARC, not only a designated terrorist organization by the U.S. and EU, but one of the world's largest drug trafficking organizations. In the same conversation he offered to supply the FARC with drones that could carry enough explosives to destroy the U.S.-financed radar stations in Colombia that track illicit aircraft movements.

Bout was the tangible embodiment of the criminal-terrorist nexus, able to deal across ideological, religious, and legal boundaries in ways that others have followed, albeit on a smaller scale. His arrest shows that it is possible to design effective legal, intelligence, and law enforcement strategies for dealing with the complex web of relationships and supply networks that fuel the nexus.

Identifying and knocking out shadow facilitators is a new

strategy, primarily being pursued by the DEA. When a facilitator falls or an operation is dismantled, the criminal, terrorist, and rogue clients do not disintegrate. However, such actions are extremely disruptive. Key clients find their supply lines damaged, normal business channels cut off, and the cost of doing business much more costly in both time and money. Other facilitator organizations that are smaller and less efficient, with less access to sophisticated weapons, can and do move into the void. But the result is a more fragmented, more vulnerable organization.

In the ongoing efforts to combat terrorism, organized crime, and the nexus among disparate criminal and terrorist organizations, there is no silver bullet. Targeting shadow facilitators is one of most effective ways of degrading the capacities of several organizations at once. Follow-up pressure on the successor organizations is then necessary to further degrade these actors. The Bout arrest shows that the first step can be effectively taken. It remains to be seen if there is sufficient long-range focus and political will to take further actions.

Animal Rights Activist Threatens Mayor

After a roaming wild cougar was shot dead in northern Chicago on April 14 by law enforcement, Mayor Richard M. Daley received vicious and threatening letters; ten days later, an arson fire was set near Daley's vacation home in Grand Beach, Michigan.[173] The threats that Mayor Daley received were linked to the cougar's death, as an FBI special agent told the press that "a number of letters were received at various locations throughout the metropolitan area blaming Mayor Daley and others for what the writer called the unnecessary death of the cougar, and threatening to take revenge against the mayor and other individuals."[174] The media reported that one letter "included rants against the mayor, his wife and adult children. It also refers to [Daley's] late son, Kevin, who died of spina binfida as a toddler more than 25 years ago. The author reportedly wrote 'f--- your dead son.'"[175]

---

173. Kari Lydersen, "Arson Near Chicago Mayor's Home May Be Linked to Cougar's Killing," *Washington Post*, May 25, 2008.
174. Ibid.
175. Ben Bradley, "Letter Sent to Mayor Disrespects Late Son," *ABC News*, May 23, 2008.

Though Daley's Michigan home was not damaged, the house of one of his neighbors was destroyed.

Animal Rights Group Launches Coordinated Attacks

In early August, a pair of near-simultaneous firebomb attacks targeted two University of California at Santa Cruz researchers. A little before 6 a.m. on August 2, a molecular biologist's home was hit by a firebomb, and the scientist and his family "escaped by ladder from the second floor."[176] Around the same time, "a second researcher's car was firebombed and destroyed. The car was parked outside the scientist's house on campus."[177]

A day before these attacks, a flier was posted at a Santa Cruz coffee shop listing the names of 13 university employees who worked with animals. It stated: "Animal abusers everywhere beware; we know where you live; we know where you work; we will never back down until you end your abuse."[178] A *U.S. News & World Report* blogger noted that there had been a number of incidents prior to this targeting scientists who worked with animals:

> Saturday's incidents are not the first that have targeted University of California scientists who work with animals. A number of researchers at *UCLA* have been attacked and/or harassed since 2006, leading to a lawsuit and a restraining order, and in late February, a family member of a UC-Santa Cruz scientist was assaulted. Authorities have pointed to animal rights extremists for all the acts.[179]

The coordinated attacks in Santa Cruz showed that animal rights-motivated harassment was trending in the wrong direction. Santa Cruz police captain Steve Clark commented, "There has definitely been an increase in the volume of harassment, and now we've seen an increase in the stakes of the violence that they're willing to spread in the name of this cause. This signals a new level of aggressiveness."[180]

---

176. "Two UC-Santa Cruz Researchers Victims of Firebombing," *Paper Trail*, Aug. 4, 2008.
177. Ibid.
178. Ibid.
179. Ibid.
180. John Cote, "Pro-Animal Militants Terrorizing Researchers," *San Francisco Chronicle*, Aug. 6, 2008.

"Most Dangerous Woman in the World" Apprehended

Aafia Siddiqui, an MIT graduate with a doctorate in neuroscience from Brandeis University, had long been wanted by American authorities for suspected cooperation with al-Qaeda. The FBI first placed her under surveillance in 2002 "after she ordered a flak jacket and book on explosives."[181] She returned to Pakistan in 2002, and had "not been heard of since March 2003, when she took a cab from Karachi to Islamabad to visit her mother."[182] It is believed that her name first emerged in al-Qaeda investigations when 9/11 mastermind Khalid Sheikh Mohammed mentioned her during a CIA-led interrogation. A profile in *Spiegel Online* notes Siddiqui's high profile among terrorist hunters:

> [S]he was the most-wanted woman in the world for four years. The FBI considered her so dangerous that former Attorney General John Ashcroft placed her—the only woman—on his "Deadly Seven" list. The American press nicknamed Siddiqui the terrorist organization al-Qaida's "Mata Hari" and its "female genius." She's believed to have raised money for al-Qaida by collecting donations and smuggling diamonds. "She is the most important catch in five years," former CIA terrorist hunter John Kiriakou said when she was apprehended.[183]

Though Siddiqui has claimed that she was abducted by the CIA and held in a secret prison,[184] the U.S. government has stated that she was first taken into custody by the Afghan National Police in July 2008 after they observed her acting suspiciously outside the Ghazni governor's compound. At the time of her arrest, she had on her "handwritten notes that referred to a 'mass casualty attack' and that listed various locations in the United States, including Plum Island, the Empire State Building, the Statue of Liberty, Wall Street, and the Brooklyn Bridge."[185] She also had notes referring to the construction of dirty bombs, as well as chemical and biological weapons. Siddiqui was

---

181. "Female 'Terror' Scientist Aafia Siddiqui Facing U.S. Court After Extradition," *Times* (London), Aug. 5, 2008.
182. Ibid.
183. Juliane von Mittelstaedt, "The Most Dangerous Woman in the World," *Spiegel Online* (Germany), Nov. 27, 2008.
184. The CIA vigorously denies this claim. Michael Scheuer, who headed the CIA's bin Laden unit in the 1990s, said bluntly: ""We never arrested or imprisoned a woman. She is a liar." Ibid.
185. *United States v. Siddiqui*, Indictment (S.D.N.Y. 2008), ¶ 3.

then transferred to U.S. custody.

Despite Siddiqui's allegedly longstanding connection to al-Qaeda, her later indictment in New York stemmed solely from an attack on U.S. military personnel after she was transferred to American custody. According to the Department of Justice:

> The personnel entered a second floor meeting room—unaware that Siddiqui was being held there, unsecured, behind a curtain. The Warrant Officer took a seat and placed his United States Army M-4 rifle on the floor next to the curtain. Shortly after the meeting began, the Captain heard a woman yell from the curtain and, when he turned, saw Siddiqui holding the Warrant Officer's rifle and pointing it directly at the Captain. Siddiqui said, "May the blood of [unintelligible] be directly on your [unintelligible, possibly head or hands]." The interpreter seated closest to Siddiqui lunged at her and pushed the rifle away as Siddiqui pulled the trigger. Siddiqui fired at least two shots but no one was hit. The Warrant Officer returned fire with a 9 mm service pistol and fired approximately two rounds at Siddiqui's torso, hitting her at least once.[186]

She currently faces trial in the United States.

Arizona Man Arrested for Making False Statements to the FBI

On August 20, Akram Musa Abdallah was arrested on charges of lying to the FBI.[187] His indictment states that in January 2007 the "defendant represented that he was not involved in fund raising activities for the Holy Land Foundation for Relief & Development … when, in fact, between approximately 1994 and 1997, defendant was involved in fund raising activities."[188] The Holy Land Foundation had previously been named a specially designated global terrorist entity by the U.S. Treasury Department for its support of the Palestinian terrorist group Hamas, and five of its leaders were ultimately convicted in November 2008 for providing material support to Hamas.

---

186. U.S. Department of Justice, Press Release, "Aafia Siddiqui Arrested for Attempting to Kill United States Officers in Afghanistan," Aug. 4, 2008.

187. Office of the United States Attorney, District of Arizona, Press Release, "Mesa Man Charged For Lying to the FBI," Aug. 21, 2008.

188. *United States v. Abdallah*, Indictment, CR08-0947 (D. Ariz., Aug. 19, 2008).

Escaped Convict Killed in Somalia

Seattle-area barber Ruben Shumpert, a convert to Islam, pled guilty to a weapons charge and transferring counterfeit currency in late 2006, in a case that was "deeply colored by allegations of terrorism."[189] However, just before he was to be sentenced, Shumpert called an FBI agent who worked his case and said that he would not appear in court:

> Shumpert said he was in Somalia, the lawless East African nation far beyond the reach of the U.S. government. In a second taunting phone call to the FBI, according to prosecutors, Shumpert said he and his associates "would destroy everything the United States stood for." As he spoke, the FBI agent said, a crowd in the background chanted "Allah Akbar"—the Arabic phrase meaning "God is Great" that is sometimes used to cheer someone on, or as a terrorist battle cry.[190]

Sometime before October 1, Shumpert was killed in a missile strike targeting terrorists in Somalia. In the aftermath of his death, the terrorist group Shahaab al-Mujahideen released a biography of Shumpert hailing him as a martyr.[191]

Shirwa Ahmed and the Missing Somalis

Shirwa Ahmed, a naturalized U.S. citizen from Minnesota, also liaised with Somalia's Shabaab al-Mujahideen. In October, he blew himself up in a suicide bombing that killed twenty-nine people in northern Somalia. According to a family friend, his sister received a phone call from Ahmed the day before the attack saying that she wouldn't see him again; the following day, "someone else called from Somalia to say he had 'gone to paradise' as a martyr for Islam."[192]

Ahmed came to the U.S. with his family in 1995 as a young teenager, and graduated from Minneapolis's Roosevelt High School in 1999.[193] He displayed a noticeable increase in religiosity as he

---

189. Jeanne Meserve & Mike M. Ahlers, "Seattle Case Raises Questions About War on Terror," *CNN*, Dec. 18, 2006.
190. Ibid.
191. "Shabaab Martyr Biography of American Convert," SITE Intelligence Group, Oct. 4, 2008.
192. Bob Drogin, "Young Men Vanish into Somalia, Stirring Fears of Terrorist Recruitment," *Los Angeles Times*, Jan. 18, 2009.
193. James Walsh et al., "Missing Twin Cities Somalis, Terror Ties Probed," *Star Tribune* (Minneapolis-St. Paul), Nov. 25, 2008.

radicalized. As a local media outlet reported, "[h]is high school pictures show a clean cut young man and neighbors at his Minneapolis apartment say lately 26-year-old Shirwa Ahmed had a thick beard."[194]

Shirwa Ahmed was not the only one: dozens of young men in the Minneapolis-St. Paul area disappeared over the course of 2008, causing community members and U.S. intelligence officials to fear that they are joining jihadist groups in Somalia. Ahmed's death drew attention to this issue, and by December 2008 the Twin Cities media reported that a number of other young Somali men—estimates ranged from six to 40—had disappeared from the area. Multiple sources within the local Somali community and U.S. government feared that these men may have returned to Somalia to train, or to participate in jihad against the country's secular transitional federal government (TFG).

"I've come across 10 to 15 mothers crying because their sons are missing," said Omar Jamal, executive director of the Minneapolis-based Somali Justice Advocacy Center.[195] Jamal said the Somali community has seen young men disappear in a number of countries across the world, including Canada, the Netherlands and Australia. Multiple sources within the Somali community corroborated this account. For example, Dahir Jibreel, who previously served as the TFG's permanent secretary in charge of international cooperation, said, "Other young Somalis went missing in Europe, Saudi Arabia and elsewhere."[196] Jibreel said many of the disappearances occurred simultaneously.

Abdiweli Ali, an associate professor of economics at Niagara University and a former adviser to the TFG, said young Somalis are being targeted for indoctrination. "There's a huge underclass," he said, "and the kids get involved in gangs and drugs. So every time a kid goes to hang out in the mosque, the parents see that as good. They encourage their kids to go to after-school programs with religion, to youth groups at the mosque."[197] The youths are susceptible to "brainwashing," Ali said. "They are very young, susceptible to any kind of indoctrination. All you need is one rogue imam who tells them the wrong things, and they are susceptible to that."

---

194.   Esme Murphy, "MN Man Possibly Behind Recruiting Somali Terrorists," *WCCO.com*, Nov. 26, 2008.
195.   Author telephone interview with Omar Jamal, executive director of the Somali Justice Advocacy Center, Dec. 2008.
196.   Author telephone interview with Dahir Jibreel, Dec. 2008.
197.   Author telephone interview with Abdiweli Ali, Dec. 2008.

In 2009, there were further reports of Somalis going missing in Columbus, Ohio, and Boston.

From Minnesota to Shabelle: Somalis Return to the Homeland to Participate in Jihad
By Reuven Paz

On June 6, 2006, the Minnesota chapter of the Muslim American Society issued an Islamic ruling (*fatwa*) proclaiming that Islamic law forbids taxi drivers from carrying passengers who have alcohol on them "because it involves cooperating in sin according to Islam." During 2007, many Somali taxi drivers refused to carry such passengers; this drew great attention to the community of Somali immigrants in North America in general, and in Minnesota in particular. Investigations by U.S. authorities, the media, and local social workers suggested a process of religious radicalization among young Somalis, most of them refugees, who came to the U.S. and Canada in the 1990s.

In the second half of 2008, about twenty parents or family members of young Somalis from the United States reported that their sons had disappeared. Soon, both reports and rumors began to emerge claiming that these youngsters had gone to Somalia to join jihadi groups there, primarily the pro-al-Qaeda Mujahidin Youth Movement (also known as Shabaab), which is the largest group of jihadi insurgents in the war-torn country, and the group that most threatens efforts to achieve stability in Somalia.

On January 8, 2008, a number of jihadi forums posted a manifesto written by an American Muslim calling himself Abu Mansour al-Amriki, who called for Muslim emigrants to join Shabaab.

In October 2008, Shabaab published its first magazine on the Internet—*Millat (the religion of) Ibrahim*—issued by the "Al-Zarqawi Center for Studies and Research, which belongs to the media section of the Mujahidin Youth Movement." The "Immigrants' Forum" section of the magazine featured the story of a Muslim convert from the United States, Ruben Shumpert, who died in Somalia. The story begins with his childhood in Seattle, and ends with how he was killed in a U.S. missile strike in Somalia.

The same month, two suicide bombers carried out an attack against government facilities in Somalia. According to official statements by the FBI, one of them—Shirwa Ahmed—was a naturalized American citizen from Minnesota's Twin Cities, who had arrived in the U.S. along with his family in 1996. The FBI returned his body to Minneapolis, where he was given a Muslim burial.

In April 2009, a young Somali who came from the U.S., Umar Muhammad Jama, was arrested by Somalia's Ahlu Sunnah wal Jama'a group while on his way to carry out a suicide operation.

This phenomenon of Somali youth, most of whom came to the U.S. as children and grew up in America—but were recruited or volunteered to return to Somalia to join the jihadi insurgency's most extreme pro-al-Qaeda group—points to several significant and related elements:

A. In many cases, Muslim immigrants to Western countries remain emotionally attached to their homeland, especially if they live as a closed group. We can observe this among old communities in Europe as well, and even among second and third generations of immigrants. Many of the Somalis in North America also came as political refugees. This means that in part, they are still hoping for stability in the homeland in order to return there. Many of them view their time in America as temporary, a stopping point on their journey home.

B. Somali youth in the U.S. have proven vulnerable to Islamic preaching that provides them the identity for which they are searching. The Islamic atmosphere in their communities in the Twin Cities has been preserved and developed by the apparatus affiliated with the U.S. Muslim Brotherhood. However, some Somali youths are attracted by the combination of extreme Salafism and Somali nationalism, and wish to return to what they consider the real homeland to join the fight to establish a jihadi-Salafi Somali state.

C. In the past two years, Somalia became one of the cornerstones of global jihadi fights, affiliated with and encouraged by al-Qaeda. Shabaab emerged as an independent force after it split from its mother movement, the Islamic Courts Union. One factor pushing the split, as emphasized by Shabaab's publications, was the factions' relative openness to the acceptance of foreign volunteers. Shabaab, assisted by the propaganda and indoctrination apparatuses of Al-Qaeda and other global jihadi groups, encourages this trend of volunteers.

D. Recruiting volunteers to fight in major conflict areas is a stated strategy of the jihadi-Salafi groups. From 2003 to 2007 in Iraq, the vast majority of the pro-al-Qaeda factions' suicide bombers were non-Iraqi volunteers. This model followed the large stream of volunteers who went to Afghanistan in the 1980s to fight the Soviets. This is an essential element in building global jihadi solidarity.

The Somali community in Minnesota, which numbers about 40,000, enjoys American authorities' best efforts to ease their immigration. A system of social workers, schools, good housing, and employment acts in their favor. Nevertheless, it seems that education, better social conditions, welfare, and employment are not enough to forge a new identity. Most of the Somalis in North America came as refugees, fleeing a chaotic state. Yet Islamist radicalization has led some of them to see the fight in the old homeland as the means to regain their identity.

The case of the Somalis in North America is another demonstration of the power that jihadi-Salafi preaching can hold, either by local preachers and mosques or through the Internet.

Activists Target the Wrong Car

On November 20, a group of animal rights activists attempted to target Goran Lacan, a UCLA researcher "who used animals while investigating treatments for morbid obesity and eating disorders."[198] The activists aimed to set fire to Lacan's car, but got the wrong address. They destroyed one vehicle and damaged two others, none of which belonged to Lacan.[199] The extremist group Students and Workers for the Liberation of UCLA Primates claimed credit for the attack.

---

198. "Anti-Animal Research Group Bombs Car," *Associated Press,* Nov. 28, 2008.
199. Andrew Blankstein, "Animal Rights Extremists Target UCLA Researcher in Arson Attack," *Los Angeles Times*, Nov. 29, 2008.

TRANSNATIONAL TERRORIST GROUPS ACTIVE IN THE WEST

Some transnational terrorist groups are engaged in activities that span several Western countries. As noted in the first part of this report, when terrorist groups develop significant capacities in the West, it both increases their operational strength and builds resiliency. This section of the report discusses two significant groups that have been active across a range of Western countries, the Kurdish Workers Party (PKK) and Liberation Tigers of Tamil Eelam (LTTE).

The PKK in 2008

The Kurdish Workers Party (PKK) is a Kurdish nationalist terror group that originally professed a Marxist-Leninist ideology upon its founding in 1974. The group is primarily based in southern Turkey and northern Iraq, and uses violence to pressure Middle Eastern governments with large Kurdish populations. Turkey has been its primary focus. The PKK has primarily used Europe to raise money for its operations. The terrorist group "has a vast European propaganda and fundraising network that includes two news agencies, four television stations, thirteen radio stations, ten newspapers, nineteen periodicals, and three publishing houses. These media organizations are scattered across Europe and range from ROJ TV in Denmark to the Firat News Agency in the Netherlands."[200] The PKK has also been involved in the European drug trade and human trafficking.

PKK financial controller deported from Britain. Though the date of his apprehension is not clear, PKK financier Bozkur Selman was deported by British authorities in early 2008. British authorities "noted that Bozkur handled the funds of the organization, stating that the decision to deport him and seize his property will be a financial blow to the PKK."[201] Selman is now believed to be residing in France, "where he is entitled to legal residency following his deportation from England."[202]

Former girlfriend of PKK leader arrested in Germany. Ayfer Kaya,

---

200. Abdulkadir Onay, "PKK Criminal Networks and Fronts in Europe," *Policy Watch* #1344, Washington Institute for Near East Policy, Feb. 21, 2008.
201. "Britain Deports PKK Financial Handler," *Zaman* (Turkey), Feb. 27, 2008.
202. Ibid.

allegedly a former girlfriend of Abdullah Ocalan, was arrested by German police in March 2008 on charges of belonging to the banned PKK organization.[203] Kaya was arrested after arriving in Germany from Austria.[204] At the time, Turkey—which had two warrants for Kaya's arrest—was expected to request her extradition.[205] However, Kaya was released after Turkey failed to file necessary documents related to the extradition by a court-imposed deadline.

PKK raids arrest 29 women in Belgium. Belgian police arrested twenty-nine women in April who were accused of undergoing training with the PKK around the town of Verviers.[206] The women were arrested as part of a series of police raids on suspected PKK locations.[207] In addition to the arrests, the anti-terror police who participated in the raids seized documents and computers.[208]

Conviction of Muzaffer Ayata. In April, a German court sentenced Turkish citizen Muzaffer Ayata to three and a half years in prison for being a top leader of the banned PKK.[209] He was also convicted of threatening Kurds who refused to make contributions to the PKK. During sentencing, the judge said that Ayata was one of the top three PKK leaders operating in German cities, and that he is "wanted in Turkey for at least 3,000 murders, in fighting against the Turkish army."[210]

Extradition of Nedim Seven. Italy confirmed in May that PKK member Nedim Seven would be extradited to France to face money laundering charges, even though Turkey had also requested his extradition.[211] Seven, who had been arrested in Rome, was one of sixteen PKK members "detained in a key French crackdown on the terrorist group in February 2007."[212] However, the detained members were released pending trial, and several—including Seven—escaped from France. He was rearrested in Rome in October 2007 when trying to leave for Armenia.

---

203. "Purported Lover of PKK Leader Ocalan Arrested," *AFP*, Mar. 13, 2008.
204. "Former Girlfriend of PKK Leader Ocalan Detained in Germany," *Trend News* (Azerbaijan), Mar. 13, 2008.
205. "Ex-Girlfriend of PKK Leader Ocalan Detained in Germany," *World Bulletin*, Mar. 13, 2008.
206. "Belgian Police Raid PKK Offices," *International News* (Pakistan), Apr. 6, 2008.
207. "Belgium Police Launch Raid on Turkish PKK Rebel Suspects," *AFP*, Apr. 4, 2008.
208. "Belgian Police Raid PKK Offices," *International News*.
209. "German Court Jails PKK Official," *AFP*, Apr. 12, 2008.
210. Ibid.
211. Ali Ihsan Aydin, "Italy to Extradite Senior PKK Leader to France Instead of Turkey," *Zaman* (Turkey), May 3, 2008.
212. Ibid.

ROJ TV ban. On June 19, Germany banned the television station ROJ TV, accusing the station of being "a mouthpiece of the PKK."[213] German officials claimed that "ROJ TV programs glorify PKK guerilla fighters, encourage Kurds to join the PKK and incite violence."[214] They also dissolved ROJ's production company, and prohibited its Danish-based parent company from operating in Germany. PKK-affiliated television stations have also been banned in France and the U.K., but ROJ TV continues to broadcast in Denmark.

German arrest of suspected PKK official. In July, German police arrested a Turk identified as "Hueseyin A.," who was suspected of leading the PKK's German branch.[215] He was also accused "of having forced a 21-year-old woman to have an abortion in August 2007, after she became pregnant by a leading PKK official in the southwestern city of Stuttgart."[216] In December, he was formally charged with membership in a criminal organization, and could face a maximum of five years imprisonment.[217]

Eleven to stand trial over firebomb attacks in France. In July, eleven suspected PKK members were ordered to stand trial in France, "charged with financing terrorism and bombing property."[218] The charges stemmed from a series of firebomb attacks directed against Turkish cafes and a cultural center in Bordeaux and Marseille in 2007.[219] The attacks injured a number of people, including causing severe burn damage. A twelfth suspect, who was a minor at the time of the attacks, was sent to juvenile court. The trial for the eleven adults charged commenced in December.

Swiss crackdown on PKK fundraising. The Swiss government launched a crackdown in November following a series of attacks against Turkish properties (including cafes, travel agencies, and others) that was blamed on the PKK.[220] Though the PKK is not banned in Switzerland due to lack of a legal mechanism for doing so, Switzerland's president

---

213. "Germany Bans PKK Affiliated-Satellite Broadcaster Roj TV," *Zaman* (Turkey), June 26, 2008.
214. Guy Degen, "Kurdish ROJ TV Sparks Debate," *Deutsche World* (Germany), Dec. 10, 2008.
215. "German Police Arrest Suspected PKK Official," *Reuters*, July 22, 2008.
216. Ibid.
217. "German Authorities Charge PKK Suspect," *Associated Press*, Jan. 8, 2009.
218. "Suspected PKK Members to Stand Trial in France," *Associated Press*, July 30, 2008.
219. "French Court to Try 11 Kurds Over Attacks in France," *AFP*, July 30, 2008.
220. "Switzerland Declares Measures Against PKK," *Zaman* (Turkey), Nov. 7, 2008.

called the organization "dangerous" during a trip to Turkey.[221] The Swiss government "banned fundraising events due to be held at Kurdish celebrations, and also "applied a more restrictive policy on demonstration permits." Turkey has frequently criticized Switzerland "for not taking enough steps to combat the PKK, whose members are accused of laundering money in Swiss banks."[222]

London raids on PKK associations. In December, British police carried out a number of coordinated raids on PKK affiliated associations in London.[223] Authorities detained suspected PKK members, including an official with one of the associations. Individuals who were detained could face charges for membership in a terrorist organization, terrorist financing, or propagandizing on a terrorist organization's behalf. According to reports, the operations targeted "clubs providing financial support and man power to the PKK."[224]

Liberation Tigers of Tamil Eelam (LTTE)

The Liberation Tigers of Tamil Eelam (LTTE) was formed in 1983 to fight for a separate Tamil homeland in Sri Lanka. Since then, the group became truly transnational in scope, with activities in multiple countries and multiple continents. Though LTTE experienced a dramatic military defeat in 2009, many analysts believe that the transnational support network it built means that the group will be with us for years to come.

Some LTTE supporters have engaged in terrorist financing. For example, Canadian citizen Prapaharan Thambithurai was charged in March for raising money for the LTTE.[225] French authorities arrested two top LTTE leaders in their country who had been involved in "fund raising activities and money laundering for the LTTE."[226]

Other supporters have attempted to send LTTE military hardware. Four men in Britain were charged with conspiring to receive equipment to support LTTE; they were "accused of possessing equipment including radios, computers and high-power magnets

221. "Couchepin Explains PKK Crackdown," *Swissinfo.ch*, Nov. 9, 2008.
222. Emrullah Uslu, "Turkey Urges International Cooperation in Its Struggle Against Kurdish Militants," *Terrorism Focus*, The Jamestown Foundation, Nov. 19, 2008.
223. "PKK Operation in Britain," *TRT World* (Turkey), Dec. 23, 2008.
224. "Britain Detains Several PKK Terrorists in London," *Hurriyet* (Turkey), Dec. 23, 2008.
225. "Canada Makes First Terror Financing Charge," *UPI*, Mar. 18, 2008.
226. "Internal Fissures Widen in LTTE as Forces Gain Ground in North," *Daily News* (Sri Lanka), June 6, 2008.

for terrorism."[227] A number of individuals were also sentenced by a federal court based Baltimore for their efforts to provide hardware to LTTE. These include Sri Lankan citizen Thirunavukarasu Varatharasa, who was sentenced to 57 months imprisonment by a U.S. court after pleading guilty to providing material support to LTTE, including attempting to export "state-of-the-art firearms, machine guns and ammunition, surface to air missiles, night vision goggles and other military weapons to the Liberation Tigers of Tamil Eelam."[228] Similarly, the court sentenced retired Indonesian Marine Corps General Erick Wotulo for attempting to "export state-of-the-art firearms, machine guns and ammunition, surface to air missiles, night vision goggles and other military weapons to the Liberation Tigers of Tamil Eelam."[229]

LTTE networks were active in a number of other Western countries. Italy arrested 33 suspected LTTE members in June, and charged them with belonging to the outlawed group.[230] Italian authorities expressed hopes that in doing so, they had "effectively dismantled the Tamil Tiger fundraising network in Italy."[231] There was also an LTTE-related arrest in Australia.[232]

If the LTTE is able to make a comeback, the networks it has built in the West will almost certainly be a part of that story.

The New Leader of the LTTE
By Rohan Gunaratna

The LTTE has been militarily defeated, but it maintains a state of the art propaganda, fundraising, procurement, and shipping infrastructure overseas—particularly in the West. The LTTE has offices and cells in about 60 countries. About a million Sri Lankan

---

227. "Four on Tamil Tiger Terror Charges," *Daily Express* (U.K.), May 8, 2008.
228. U.S. Department of Justice, Press Release, "Sri Lankan Man Sentenced to 57 Months for Conspiracy to Provide Material Support to a Foreign Terrorist Organization and Attempted Export of Arms," Jan. 3, 2008.
229. U.S. Department of Justice, Press Release, "Indonesian Man Sentenced in Conspiracy to Provide Material Support to a Foreign Terrorist Organization and Money Laundering," July 10, 2008.
230. "Italy Arrests 33 Tamils Over LTTE Links," *Daily Times* (Pakistan), June 19, 2008.
231. "Italy Holds 'Tamil Tiger' Members," *BBC News*, June 18, 2008.
232. "Melbourne Business College Chief Arrested after FBI tipoff over Tamil Tiger Terror Offences," *Australian*, July 16, 2008.

Tamils live overseas, allowing the LTTE to establish a significant overseas presence. For a quarter century, the LTTE raised funds, procured supplies and transported them to Sri Lanka to support LTTE's campaign of violence. The shadowy leader responsible for building that clandestine network, Kumaran Pathmanathan (also known as KP), was appointed as the new leader of the LTTE in May 2009.

KP was the principal facilitator and enabler that transformed the LTTE into one of the world's most dangerous terrorist groups. Although KP is not a public figure, he is well known to international security and intelligence services in both the East and West. Wanted for crimes in several countries—including India, Malaysia, and Sri Lanka—K.P. is of security interest worldwide. Like Velupillai Prabhakaran in the past, KP will never be able to surface. To engage the services of a range of officials and specialists, KP bribed government officials and paid for other services. In the intelligence world, K.P. earned the same notoriety of Khalid Sheikh Mohammed, the mastermind of al Qaeda's 9/11 operation.

Who is KP?

Born in Jaffna in northern Sri Lanka on April 6, 1955, KP was educated in Sri Lanka. He entered the University of Jaffna in the mid 1970s. He has been involved with terrorist groups since the late 1970s. KP developed a close relationship with LTTE leader Velupillai Prabhakaran. Since India's foreign intelligence service, the Research and Analysis Wing (RAW), supported the LTTE from August 1983 to July 1987, KP enjoyed the immunity of the government of India. Indian intelligence officers facilitated his activities not only in India but also overseas. India's sponsorship of the LTTE gave KP a head start in building a state-of-the-art network in a short period of time.

Since the LTTE was a known terrorist group, KP operated under a dozen aliases. He also used multiple passports, including Sri Lankan, Indian, Swiss, Malaysian, and Egyptian. Since the early 1980s, KP operated from India (Madras and Bombay), Malaysia (Penang and Kuala Lumpur), and Thailand (Bangkok and Chiang Mai). He also visited the U.S., Europe, and the Middle East to procure weapons and dual-use technologies. As the LTTE is a well-known terrorist group, KP operated through three dozen LTTE front, cover, and sympathetic organizations.

KP's Modus Operandi

Willing to take risks and work long hours, KP earned the trust of Prabhakaran and his family, as well as other LTTE leaders. When Prabhakaran married Madhivadhani in Madras, KP sat next to Prabhakaran. Initially LTTE chartered ships, but after the group was duped KP was entrusted with building LTTE's own shipping fleet. KP appointed and supervised Sri Lankan Tamils who volunteered to serve as LTTE accountants and bankers, procurement officers, ship captains, and crew. The ships managed by KP initially transported the weapons to Indian waters, and thereafter to the Sri Lankan waters. Using trawlers, LTTE transported the weapons and related technologies to shore. To manage the operation, KP traveled extensively worldwide building a financial, procurement, and shipping network.

A few professional Tamils in Washington, D.C., Maryland, and New York visited arms exhibitions on KP's behalf. KP was so daring that he even visited the U.S. to procure weapons. A master of disguise and forgery, KP was able to escape the attention of law enforcement and security and intelligence services. A former accountant of the LTTE said that whenever he met with KP at an airport, KP recognized him—and not vice versa.

KP's Contribution

KP enabled the LTTE to establish itself as one of the world's most dangerous terrorist groups. KP procured the explosives used by LTTE to build the first suicide jacket in 1991, a technology that would be copied by two dozen terrorist groups worldwide. The network built by KP facilitated the LTTE to assassinate Rajiv Gandhi, a former Prime Minister of India. Similarly, 50 tons of TNT and 10 tons of RDX (the plastic explosive) purchased by KP from the Rubezone chemical plant in the Ukraine in 1994 killed thousands of civilians and soldiers. No terrorist group in history had ever purchased such a large quantity of explosives.

In appreciation of his contribution to the LTTE, Prabhakaran appointed KP to the Central Committee of the LTTE and made him the Secretary of LTTE's International Affairs Division. For nearly three decades, KP has been the *de facto*—and now the *de jure*—head of the LTTE international network. After the death of Prabhakaran and the core leadership in May 2009, KP has emerged as his successor. If KP survives, the threat from LTTE will persist.

Securing Sri Lanka

Sri Lanka will face many challenges in the coming years. Nonetheless, the events of the last thirty years demonstrate that Sri Lanka is a resilient nation. Even if ten organizations like the LTTE emerge, the government will be able to neutralize the threat. Although the LTTE in Sri Lanka is dead, there will be efforts by the vast LTTE network overseas to revive violence.

As long as support for LTTE persists overseas, Sri Lanka will remain under threat. To meet these threats, it is paramount for Sri Lanka to build a powerful security and intelligence service. By investing in recruiting and training the best minds, future governments will be able to detect threats and neutralize them before they manifest. Sri Lanka will also have to build its capacity to respond to developments overseas.

SECTION III.
LANDMARK CASES

Landmark criminal cases in 2008 can be roughly divided into five categories. The first category is cases that have been brought for actual terrorist plots and operational activity. The next three categories are cases prosecuting logistical or material support of terrorism; terrorist propaganda and recruitment; and membership in a terrorist organization. Finally, authorities have often *undercharged* in terrorism cases. That is, when there is a clear suspicion of terrorist activity, authorities will sometimes bring lesser charges (for criminal activity, for example) as a means of shutting down the terrorist activity without actually bringing a terrorism-related charge. Each of these categories will be examined in turn.

TERRORIST PLOTS AND OPERATIONAL ACTIVITY

There were a number of successful prosecutions for terrorist plots and operational activity in 2008, as prosecutors secured several key convictions. One notable trend in 2008, however, was convictions being overturned on appeal due to evidentiary issues. In part, the convictions being overturned on appeal demonstrate the high evidentiary bar that prosecutors need to meet to prove their case in terrorism trials in many Western countries.

Prosecution Successes

In Australia, the prosecution secured a conviction of seven men who were arrested in 2005 as part of Operation Pendennis, and charged with plotting to carry out a range of jihadi-inspired terrorist attacks in Sydney and Melbourne. Targets allegedly included the finals of a soccer championship and the Crown Casino.[233] On September 15 and 16, 2008, the group members were found guilty of a variety of terrorism-related offences. The group was led by Melbourne cleric Abdul Nacer Benbrika, who became the first Australian to be found guilty of directing a homegrown terrorist organization.[234]

During the trial, evidence submitted to the court explained how Benbrika's group functioned:

> Among the 480 conversations played to the court obtained through listening devices or telephone intercepts was a conversation about whether then prime minister John Howard should die for killing innocent Muslims. During the trial, the jury was told Benbrika had created a terrorist organisation bent on violent jihad with plans to bomb the 2005 AFL Grand Final or busy train stations. The group organised meetings, some private in a group member's garage or home, others in more open locations such as the Moreland Town Hall or a public park. The group had a "consultative committee" that acted as a leadership group, organising to raise funds for the group's activities. Prosecutors alleged several men in the organisation had defined roles, such as a security officer and treasurer, and certain members were involved in a car stealing racket to raise money.[235]

Aimen Joud, Abdullah Merhi, Ahmed Raad, Ezzit Raad, Fadl Sayadi, and Amer Haddara were also found guilty of membership in a terrorist organization.

---

233. Peter Gregory, "Witness Denies Making Up Discussion Over MCG Attack," *The Age* (Australia), Apr. 18, 2008.
234. Michael Ruffles, "Six Found Guilty in Terrorist Trial," *Canberra Times* (Australia), Sept. 15, 2008.
235. Ibid.

However, the jury could not reach a verdict on Shane Kent.[236] Kent, a convert to Islam, allegedly traveled to Pakistan in 2001 to undertake terrorist training.[237] He faces retrial for being a member of a terrorist group, as well as two other terrorism-related charges.[238] The court also acquitted Shouie Hammoud, Bassam Raad, Majid Raad, and Hany Taha.[239]

Another prosecutorial success, in Canada, was the conviction of Mohammad Momin Khawaja, the first person charged under the country's anti-terrorism laws. On October 29, Khawaja was found guilty on seven different terrorism charges. The Canadian press has summarized his involvement in a 2004 plot to detonate a number of fertilizer bombs in Britain:

> [Khawaja] built a remote-control device to trigger the explosions, which were never carried out, his trial heard.... [Justice Douglas] Rutherford said proof that Khawaja was working actively with the London group could be found in the evidence, which included intercepted e-mails, a trip for training in Pakistan and money transfers. "Momin Khawaja was aware of the group's purposes, and whether he considered them terrorism or not, he assisted the group in many ways in the pursuit of its terrorist objective," Rutherford wrote in his judgment. "It matters not whether any terrorist activity was actually carried out."[240]

However, Justice Rutherford found reasonable doubt over whether "Khawaja knew the exact details of a plot to bomb British buildings and natural gas lines when he built the remote-control device that has become known as the Hi-Fi Digimonster."[241] This reasonable doubt allowed greater leniency for the charges of building a remote-

236. Norrie Ross, "Jury Finds Amer Haddara Guilty of Terror Cell Membership," *Herald Sun* (Australia), Sept. 16, 2008.
237. Sally Neighbor, "Aussies Schooled by al-Qa'ida," *Australian*, Nov. 9, 2005.
238. Gary Hughes, "Bailed Muslim Gang Suspect 'Swore Allegiance to Osama,'" *Australian*, Oct. 24, 2008.
239. Gary Hughes, "Four in Clear and Eager to Part Company," *Australian*, Sept. 16, 2008.
240. "Khawaja Found Guilty in Terrorism Trial," *CBC News* (Canada), Oct. 29, 2008. For Justice Rutherford's full opinion, see *Her Majesty the Queen v. Khawaja*, No. 04-G30282 (Ontario Superior Ct. of Justice, Oct. 29, 2008).
241. "Khawaja Found Guilty in Terrorism Trial," *CBC News*.

control trigger device for the bombs.

Two Danish Muslims were sentenced on October 21 for producing explosives with the intent of carrying out an attack. Though the two men were not named by the court, the Danish press identified them as Hammad Khurshid and Abdoulghani Tohki.[242] The court also found that the plot was connected to Pakistan, as Khushid visited two villages there that were known as al-Qaeda strongholds in 2007, and attended an al-Qaeda training camp in Waziristan.[243] Tokhi, who was from Afghanistan, was also told that he would have to leave Denmark upon the completion of his prison term. In a rather lame defense, Khurshid and Tohki claimed that they were planning to use Acetone peroxide (the highly unstable TATP) for fireworks.

In Germany, Lebanese engineering student Youssef Muhammad el-Hajdib was sentenced to life imprisonment in December. El-Hajdib, also known as the "Suitcase Bomber of Cologne," was convicted of multiple attempted murder charges after leaving two suitcase bombs on trains in Cologne in July 2006. The bombs failed to explode.[244] Accomplice Jihad Hamad was also convicted in a Lebanese court, and sentenced to 12 years of imprisonment with hard labor.[245]

British prosecutors experienced a remarkable degree of success over the course of 2008. They secured key convictions of members of a terrorist cell based in Birmingham that was planning to kidnap and behead a Muslim serving as a British army officer. The plot was designed to deter Muslims from joining the British military; as the prosecutor explained, "this atrocity would be filmed ... and the film released to cause panic and fear within the British armed forces and the wider public."[246]

After being convicted for his role in the plot, cell leader Parvis Khan was sentenced to life in prison.[247] (He was also found guilty of

---

242. Kim McLaughlin, "Danish Court Convicts Two of Planning Bomb Attack," *Reuters*, Oct. 21, 2008.
243. Ibid.
244. Nicholas Kulish, "Life Sentence for Failed Bomb Attempt in Germany," *New York Times*, Dec. 12, 2008.
245. "Lebanese Man Sentenced in Bomb Attempt," *Beirut Times*, Dec. 18, 2007.
246. Alan Thompson, "Fanatic's Beheading Plot" *Manchester Evening News* (Manchester, U.K.), Jan. 29, 2008.
247. West Midlands Police, Press Release, "Birmingham Counter Terrorism Trial Concludes at Leicester Crown Court," Feb. 18, 2008.

sending equipment to terrorists on the Pakistan-Afghanistan border and possessing material of use to terrorists.) Four other members of the cell were found guilty on various charges, including assisting in the commission of acts of terrorism and failing to report the intended plot.[248] These members included Zahoor Iqbal (who received seven years), Mohammed Irfan (four years), Hamid Elasmar (three years and four months), and Basisiru Gassama (two years).[249] One of the accused, Amjad Mahmood, was found not guilty on all charges, including failure to alert the authorities about the plot.

British prosecutors independently won another conviction related to the Birmingham area. Syrian-born Hassan Muhammed Sabri Al Tabbakh was arrested in late 2007 while in possession of liquid chemicals and an MP3 player that included speeches by Osama Bin Laden, Abu Musab al-Zarqawi, and Sheikh Omar Abdul-Rahman, as well as a number of nasheeds (Islamic songs), one of which had the chorus "this is the meaning of terrorism."[250] Like the two Danish Muslims found with TATP, Al Tabbakh claimed that he had intended to make fireworks. His claim met with similar success, as he was found guilty of compiling bomb-making instructions and stockpiling chemicals for a device. At Al Tabbakh's sentencing, Judge Frank Chapman said his materials were "third rate," but still had "great potential for destruction, injury and death."[251]

One of Britain's biggest prosecutorial successes in 2008 came with the conviction and sentencing of Aabid Khan, Sultan Muhammad, and Hammaad Munshi, who were arrested as part of the counterterrorist effort Operation Praline. The group leader, Aabid Khan, succeeded in recruiting a number of young people to his jihadist cause, "using internet chat to lure them in then incite them to fight."[252] One such youth whom Khan recruited was Munshi, who became Britain's youngest convicted terrorist; he was only sixteen at the time of his arrest.

---

248. David Batty, "Ringleader of Beheading Plot Jailed for Life," *Guardian* (U.K.), Feb. 18, 2008.
249. West Midlands Police, Press Release, "Birmingham Counter Terrorism Trial Concludes at Leicester Crown Court," Feb. 18, 2008.
250. Duncan Gardham, "Terrorist Bomb Maker Hassan Tabbakh Jailed for Seven Years," *Telegraph* (U.K.), July 30, 2008.
251. Ibid.
252. Crown Prosecution Services, Press Release, "Terrorist 'Mr Fix-It' Convicted with Two Others of Terrorism Offences," Aug. 18, 2008.

At Khan's sentencing, Judge Timothy Pontius noted that the store of material captured by police upon his arrest was among the "largest and most extensive ever discovered, providing vast precise information and instruction as to how to carry out terrorist activity."[253] Judge Pontius said that the most chilling of Khan's material was a "folder demonstrating in careful, methodical and lethal detail the step by step instructions of how to make a suicide bombers' vest or belt packed with ball bearings and explosives."[254] The *Guardian* reported:

> Anti-terror officers also found handbooks on explosives and poisons, information about transport systems in the UK and US and guidelines for "beating and killing hostages" and planning assassinations. They found personal details and addresses of members of the royal family, including the Queen, the Duke of Edinburgh, the Prince of Wales and the Duke of York.[255]

For his own part, Munshi seemed to be leading a double life: that of an "obedient pupil by day, and avid surfer of jihadist websites at night," when he would download detailed instructions about making explosives and killing others.[256] Munshi was in possession of two bags of ball-bearings (that might be used to make suicide vests) when he was arrested.[257]

Another British success was the conviction of a group of individuals, arrested as part of Operation Overamp, who were engaged in terrorist training inside the U.K. The case featured five convictions on a range of charges, including solicitation of murder and attending terrorist training, and three guilty pleas. Mohammed Hamid, who described himself as "Osama bin London" had "led an al-Qaeda-style terrorist cell and aspired to send his recruits to join camps in Afghanistan and East Africa."[258] He organized such outdoor activities as camping and paintball, and a jury found that "three of

---

253. James Sturcke, "Terror 'Mr Fixit' Sentenced to 12 Years," *Guardian* (U.K.), Aug. 19, 2008.
254. Ibid.
255. Ibid.
256. Nicola McCafferty, "Terrorist Who Ran X Factor for Extremists Jailed," *Daily Express* (U.K.), Aug. 19, 2008.
257. "Britain's Youngest Terrorist, Hammaad Munshi, Faces Jail after Guilty Verdict," *Times* (U.K.), Aug. 18, 2008.
258. Philippe Naughton, "'Osama bin London' Gang Guilty of Terror Training," *Times* (U.K.), Feb. 26, 2008.

these trips were terrorist training designed to recruit, groom and corrupt impressionable young Muslims."[259] Other convicted members of the group include firebrand preacher Atilla Ahmed, Kibley de Costa, Mohammad al-Figari, and Kader Ahmed. One of the accused, 41-year-old Mousa Brown, was found not guilty of all the charges against him.

Britain also secured the conviction of Bilal Talal Samad Abdulla for his role in the summer 2007 London and Glasgow car bomb attacks, although co-defendant Mohammed Asha was acquitted of both charges against him.[260] Dr. Sabeel Ahmed also pled guilty to the charge of failing to disclose information about the attack to authorities.[261]

2008 also saw both the arrest and conviction of Nathan Worrell, whose activities were motivated by his racist outlook. Detective Inspector Superintendent David Buxton, of the Counter Terrorism Unit, provided some insight into the linkages between Worrell's case and terrorist activity: "Literature found at his flat exposed his interest in creating explosives and even more concerning a number of items were recovered that could have been used to create these devices."[262] In addition to the terrorism charges, Worrell had waged a lengthy racist campaign against his neighbors, a biracial couple. Among other things, he left stickers with such slogans as: "Only inferior white women date outside their race. Be proud of your heritage. Don't be a race-mixing slut." Worrell was found guilty of possession of material for terrorist purposes and racially aggravated harassment.

In the United States, Christopher Paul pleaded guilty in June to "conspiring with others to use a weapon of mass destruction, namely explosive devices, against targets in Europe and the United States."[263] In the 1990s, Paul flew to Pakistan and Afghanistan to train and fight with al-Qaeda. Upon his return to the U.S., he began recruiting locals "with extremist intentions in order to establish a jihadist group in Ohio."[264] He traveled to and fought in a number of conflict zones,

259. Ibid.
260. U.K. Crown Prosecution Service, Press Release, "Doctor Bilal Abdulla Guilty of London and Glasgow Bomb Plot," Dec. 16, 2008.
261. Haroon Siddique, "Doctor Jailed for Concealing Airport Bomb Plot," *Guardian* (U.K.), Apr. 11, 2008.
262. "Jail for Neo-Nazi Terror Offender," *BBC News,* Dec. 12, 2008.
263. U.S. Department of Justice, Press Release, "Ohio Man Pleads Guilty to Conspiracy to Bomb Targets in Europe and the United States," June 3, 2008.
264. Ibid.

including Bosnia, and made contact with a number of international al-Qaeda leaders and Islamic radicals.

Paul conducted training operations in Ohio that were designed to replicate the training he had received in Afghanistan and Bosnia, and in 1999 he traveled to Germany to provide explosives training to an Islamic terror cell that planned to attack Americans vacationing there, as well as "U.S. embassies, diplomatic premises and military bases in Europe."[265] He also sent cell members equipment to help them forge documents for their international travels, as well as such hardware as night vision equipment and a laser range finder. He was arrested in 2007 after a four-year investigation that extended across three continents.[266] Following his guilty plea, he was sentenced to 20 years in prison.

Federal prosecutors in Ohio also secured convictions of three Toledo-area men who were working to form a terrorist cell. In the investigation, they were assisted by a retired U.S. Special Forces soldier who was approached by the men and asked for assistance in "jihad training exercises." *Time Magazine* summarized the charges against the three suspects in the case:

> The suspects, Mohammad Zaki Amawi, Marwan Othman El-Hindi and Wassam Mazloum, have all been living in the Toledo area for over a year, according to the indictment, and had studied how to build explosives and suicide vests with the intention of travel to Iraq to engage in "holy war" by attacking American soldiers. The men raised money for the operation, considered setting up a front charity organization and used an indoor shooting range for target practice, said the indictment. The men had jobs that provided potential cover for traveling to the Middle East.[267]

On June 13, 2008, a federal jury convicted all three men of conspiring to kill or maim Americans, and planning to support terrorists.

265. Ibid.
266. "U.S. Citizen Charged with Terrorist Plots," *Associated Press*, Apr. 12, 2007.
267. Brian Bennett, "How the U.S. Nabbed Alleged Terrorists in Toledo," *Time*, Feb. 21, 2006.

Also in June, University of South Florida student Ahmed Mohamed pled guilty to providing material support for terrorism.[268] This stemmed from an August 2007 incident in which Mohamed and fellow University of South Florida student Yousef Samir Megahed had their car pulled over near Goose Creek, South Carolina. Though they told the officer who pulled them over that they were headed to vacation at Sunset Beach, North Carolina, and had exited I-95 to get gas at the Goose Creek Wal-Mart, there were several problems with that story. Savannah, Georgia, where they claimed to have stopped along the way to see the beach, did not in fact have a beach; their claimed route from Tampa was so circuitous that they would have driven for 14 hours when a more direct route would have only taken five and half hours; and Goose Creek was about 50 miles from the I-95 exit.

The officer who stopped them, Corporal James Blakely of the Berkeley County, South Carolina Sheriff's Office, asked if he would find drugs, guns, or knives in the car. When Mohamed replied that he would find "just fireworks, fuses" and "small homemade rockets," Blakely countered: "Okay, you don't have a problem if I look then, right?" The subsequent search revealed safety fuses and several sections of cut PVC piping containing a potassium nitrate explosive mixture. Government forensic analysis of a laptop that Mohamed had on him at the time also revealed a video explaining how to construct a remote-controlled explosive device.

In his plea agreement, Mohamed agreed to a number of facts relating to the August 2007 arrest, and to several other matters:

> He further stipulated to his role in the creation and distribution of an instructional video on the conversion of a radio controlled toy car into a remote detonation/ ignition device. He acknowledged that "he intended the technology demonstrated in his audio/video recording to be used against those who fight for the United States" since he considered them and their allies fighting in Arab countries to be "invaders".[269]

Mohamed was sentenced to 15 years imprisonment, while

---

268. Prosecution Sentencing Memorandum, *United States v. Mohamed*, No. 8:07-CR-342-T-23MAP (M.D. Fla. Nov. 4, 2008), p. 1.
269. Ibid., p. 2.

Megahed's trial was pending as of the end of 2008.

Another U.S.-based conviction came in June 2008, when Briana Waters was convicted for her role in burning down the University's of Washington's Center for Urban Horticulture in 2001. Waters and her co-conspirators believed (incorrectly, as it turns out) that the center had been engaged in genetic engineering, which they opposed. The documents filed in the case paint an interesting picture of the cell of which Waters was a part:

> [I]n hundreds of pages of documents both sides have already filed, a fascinating picture is taking shape: of an underground environmentalist cell that the government says was known among its members by the weirdly Mafia-like tag of "the Family." In Olympia lived the head of "the Family," a man named William Rodgers who went by the moniker "Avalon," according to government briefs. He was eventually arrested in Arizona and died in his jail cell, an apparent suicide. According to the government, the cell was part of the Earth and Animal Liberation Fronts. Rodgers led divisions located in both Olympia and Eugene, Ore. In gatherings sometimes referred to as "book club meetings," members fixated on the genetic engineering of poplar trees. Genetic engineering has inflamed the passions of some environmentalists who believe it to be interfering with nature's biodiversity. The "Family" cell, the government says, staged arsons to stop it and even, at one point, "discussed whether it would be necessary to 'up the ante' and resort to assassinations." Although prosecutors don't suggest any assassinations were carried out, they say cell members, including Waters on at least one occasion, engaged in target practice.[270]

Waters was sentenced to six years in prison and ordered to pay $6 million in restitution for her role in the arson attack.[271]

On October 15, 2008, Ian Jacob Wallace pleaded guilty to

---

270. Nina Shapiro, "More Details Emerge in UW's Eco-Arson Case," *Seattle Weekly*, Feb. 5, 2008.
271. Nancy Bartley & Mike Carter, "UW Arsonist, Briana Waters, Sentenced to 6 Years," *Seattle Times*, June 20, 2008.

"attempting to cause damage in excess of $1,000 to property of the United States."[272] In the plea agreement, Wallace admitted to trying to "damage by fire" two United States Forest Service buildings on the Michigan Technological University campus in November 2001.[273] Wallace, who claimed to act on behalf of the Earth Liberation Front, acknowledged he was aware that the targeted buildings "were being used as locations for research into genetic engineering of plants."[274]

In exchange for his guilty plea and cooperation in other cases, prosecutors agreed not to charge Wallace for similar activities in Minnesota and Wisconsin.[275] He was sentenced to three years in federal prison in March 2009, and was "also ordered to pay over $1.6 million in restitution to the victims of other similar, but successful, acts of arson and property destruction in Western Wisconsin and Minnesota that he participated in between 2000 and 2002."[276]

Finally, in December 2008 five Islamic immigrants were convicted on charges of conspiracy to kill U.S. military personnel due to their plot to attack the base in Fort Dix, New Jersey.

Operational Activity With No Actual Violence

In three prosecutions that occurred in 2008, the accused made terrorist threats or even planned fake attacks, but apparently did not intend to kill anybody.

For example, British Muslim convert Nicolas Roddis was found guilty in July on terrorism charges that included placing a fake bomb on a bus. That occurred in May 2007, when a disguised Roddis left a hoax bomb inside a shopping bag on a bus with a written message inside: "There is no God but Allah and Mohammed is the messenger of Allah. God is great, god is great, god is great. Britain must be punished."[277] (Roddis may have had more on his agenda than fake attacks: when he was arrested, his apartment contained such items as acetone, hydrogen peroxide, and nails, along with bomb-making instructions.)

272. Plea Agreement, *United States v. Wallace*, No. 2:08-CR-39, (W.D. Mich. 2008), p. 1.
273. Ibid.
274. U.S. Attorney's Office, Western District of Michigan, Press Release, "Guilty Plea Entered in 2001 Eco-Terrorism Attempt at Michigan Technological University," Oct. 15, 2008.
275. Ibid.
276. U.S. Attorney's Office, Western District of Michigan, Press Release, "Sentencing in 2001 Eco-Terrorism Attempt at Michigan Technological University," Mar. 27, 2009.
277. "Muslim Convert Left Hoax Bomb Message," *Yorkshire Post* (U.K.), June 30, 2008.

British postman Jefferson Azevedo pled guilty in June to planting a hoax bomb and sending a number of hate-mail letters, some of which contained a mysterious white powder. In undertaking this campaign, Azevedo's primary motivation was apparently his racist beliefs. The BBC explains:

> The court heard that letters—postmarked "Portsmouth and IoW"—were sent to the Royal Naval Dockyard in Portsmouth, and another was posted to the Attorney General's office in London as well as Mr Blair. Two letters containing white powder were sent to St Albans Primary School in Havant. They were all signed "RAHOWA"—a racist acronym also known as Racial Holy War used in the past by white supremacists. The letters described former Home Office minister Beverley Hughes as a "race traitor" and criticised former prime minister for considering proposals to turn the former naval air station HMS Daedalus in Lee-on-the-Solent into an asylum centre.... A number of media organisations in Hampshire also received letters and 22 letters were sent to churches, mosques and restaurants.[278]

Between 2003 and 2007, Azevedo managed to send more than 150 letters to a variety of high-profile figures.

The third such case was not motivated by the defendant's animus, but rather by his own stupidity and infantilism. In the fall of 2006, Wisconsin resident Jake Brahm—who was at the time living with his parents and working part-time at a grocery store—made online threats on Internet message board 4chan warning that "America's Hiroshima" was imminent. His threat claimed:

> On Sunday, October 22nd, 2006, there will be seven "dirty" explosive devices detonated in seven different U.S. cities; Miami, New York City, Atlanta, Seattle, Houston, Oakland and Cleveland. The death toll will approach 100,000 from the initial blasts and countless other fatalities will later occur as a result from radioactive fallout.[279]

---

278. "Postman's Racist Terror Campaign," *BBC News*, June 5, 2008.
279. Indictment, *United States v. Brahm*, No. 06-8223 (D. N.J., Oct. 19, 2006), ¶ 1.

Brahm's threats were self-evidently a hoax. Nonetheless, they created a media firestorm, largely because the 2006 mid-term elections were approaching. Moreover, in this day and age, a reasonable person does not jokingly make terrorist threats. But Brahm, in his various Internet activities, was anything but a reasonable person: for example, he kept a personal blog for ten months documenting his masturbatory habits.[280] Brahm ultimately pled guilty to willfully conveying false information, and was sentenced to six months in federal prison.[281]

Group Prosecutions

Due to the complexity of large group prosecutions, there will frequently be both successes and setbacks for the prosecution in a single case over the course of a year. That was certainly the case in Canada's Toronto 18 case over the course of 2008.

On April 15, Crown prosecutors decided to stay charges filed against Ahmed Mustafa Ghany, Ibrahim Aboud, and Qayyum Abdul Jamal, and Yasim Abdi Mohamed. But on September 25, prosecutors achieved a breakthrough with the first conviction of a plot member, a twenty-year-old whose identity is protected under the Youth Criminal Justice Act (he was seventeen at the time of his arrest).[282]

Throughout his trial, the defense sought to soften the image of the defendant and the group, countering the prosecution's portrayal of a "teenage jihadi who attended two training camps" with the image of a "troubled youngster, alienated from his Hindu family for converting to Islam, who went winter camping because he was told it was a religious retreat."[283] The prosecution, however, countered these assertions through the testimony of their key witness, Mubin Shaikh, a Canadian Security Intelligence Service (CSIS) informant who infiltrated the cell. Describing what happened during the training retreats, Shaikh quipped, "We weren't there picking daisies, that's for sure."[284] Shaikh said that "the stated objective [of the group] was to cripple infrastructure and

---

280. *Jake Brahm Wangs Da Poo*, jakebrahmwangsdapoo.blogspot.com (accessed July 5, 2009).
281. U.S. Department of Justice, Press Release, "Wisconsin Man Sentenced for Conveying 'Sick' Terrorism Hoax to Detonate Dirty Bombs at U.S. Football Stadiums," June 5, 2008.
282. Melissa Leong, "Toronto 18 Youth Guilty of Terrorism," *National Post* (Canada), Sept. 26, 2008.
283. Isabel Teotonio, "Youth Canada's First Convicted Terrorist," *Toronto Star*, Sept. 26, 2008.
284. "Public Has 'Played This Off,' Alleged Bomb Plot Informant Tells Court," *CBC News* (Canada), June 10, 2008.

create chaos; to kill people with assault rifles and truck bombs."[285]

Justice John Sproat sided with the prosecution in his 94-page decision, ruling that the accused youth understood that "the camps were training for a terrorist purpose," and that "contributing materials to be used at the camp enhanced the ability of the group to conduct the training."

In France, nine men were convicted and sentenced for their roles in a terrorist cell that was suspected of planning attacks on Paris's metro and Orly Airport.[286] Ringleader Safe Bourada received the longest sentence, fifteen years.[287]

Prosecution Setbacks

Four major cases resulted in acquittals in 2008, while there were also two mistrials.

In Australia, Jill Courtney and boyfriend Hussan Kalache, accused of plotting to detonate a car bomb in the Kings Cross area of Sydney in 2006, were acquitted.[288] On February 29, the New South Wales Supreme Court jury was directed by the judge to return not guilty verdicts against the pair, as he determined there was insufficient evidence to support the charges against them.[289] After serving twenty-three months inside Mulawa women's maximum security prison as a high-risk inmate, Courtney was freed on March 1, 2008.[290] Kalache had already been imprisoned for the murder of a drug rival, and was ordered to serve the remainder of his sentence.

This case had been known as the "love bomb" case. Courtney was alleged to have planned the bombing at the request of Kalache, who promised to marry her if she carried out the attack.[291] It is believed that Kalache's motivation for the plot was retaliation for December 2005 race riots in the Sydney suburb of Cronulla.

---

285. Ibid.
286. Pierre-Antoine Souchard, "9 Convicted in Paris Terror Trial," *ABC News,* Oct. 23, 2008.
287. Ibid.
288. Marnie O'Neill, "Accused Terror Plotter's Jail Ordeal," *Sunday Telegraph* (Australia), Mar. 2, 2008.
289. "Judge's Appeal in Love Bomb Case," *Daily Telegraph* (Australia), Feb. 29, 2008.
290. O'Neill, "Accused Terror Plotter's Jail Ordeal."
291. "Sydney Bomb Plot Link to Race Riots, Murderer," *9 News* (Australia), Mar. 27, 2006.

The prosecution had built its case from intercepted telephone calls between Courtney and Kalache, in which they spoke in code about a "mission."[292] One detective said of Courtney: "For whatever reason, she's hooked up and become besotted with him [Kalache]. She's converted to Islam and apparently has his prison number tattooed on her thigh. It's a pretty sad case, she's a bit of a candle in the wind."[293]

In Norway, three individuals tried under the country's anti-terrorism laws for allegedly shooting at a synagogue and plotting to attack American and Israeli embassies in Oslo were acquitted on the grounds that prosecutors failed to prove that he was guilty of more than a serious vandalism offense.[294] In large part, ringleader Arfan Qadeer Bhatti was acquitted because "Norway's terrorism laws have a high threshold of proof."[295] He was, however, convicted on a non-terrorism charge: attempted murder for shooting at the home of the reputed head of a pyramid scheme in which he had lost money. The trial of Bhatti and the other two individuals, Andreas Bog Kristiansen and Ibrahim Oezbabacan, was the first of its kind under the country's fortified anti-terrorism laws.[296]

In Britain, teenagers Dabeer Hussain and Waris Ali were acquitted of terrorism charges after allegedly concocting a "gunpowder plot" aimed at the far-right British National Party. The British press relayed the prosecutors' explanation of the plot:

> Two Dewsbury schoolboys downloaded a 3,000-page terror manual and cooked up a 'gunpowder plot' to blow up the BNP, a court heard. Childhood pals Waris Ali and Dabeer Hussain, both 18, were found with digital copies of the Anarchist's Cookbook on their home computers. The pair also chatted on the internet about how they would spy on and bomb members of the far right political party, Leeds Crown Court was told yesterday. Ali, from Dearnley Street, Ravensthorpe, also bought several kilos of a potassium nitrate—a legal chemical which

292. "Judge's Appeal in Love Bomb Case," *Daily Telegraph.*
293. John Kidman et al., "Bizarre Plot to Bomb Sydney," *Sydney Morning Herald*, Mar. 26, 2006.
294. "Norway Terror Suspect Acquitted," *B92*, June 4, 2008.
295. Ibid.
296. "Trial Opens under Norway's Strengthened Anti-Terrorism Laws," *International Herald Tribune*, Mar. 31, 2008.

can be used in the preparation of explosives as well as fireworks—on eBay. He had also scoured the internet for information on buying hi-tech surveillance equipment, the court was told. However his naive plotting was discovered when he asked a librarian how much fertiliser could be safely stored in a person's home without raising suspicion from the authorities, the court heard.[297]

However, the jury returned an acquittal after two and a half hours of deliberation. Following the verdict, Ali blasted the prosecution: "I feel it was completely obvious once the police looked up the evidence that I had nothing to do with terrorism at all. Silly teenage chat and things I said at school were taken out of context and presented as if it was evidence that I was an extremist."[298]

Also in the U.K., animal rights activist Mel Broughton was cleared of possessing an explosive substance with intent in November. He was prosecuted as part of a "police investigation into a series of attacks aimed at preventing construction of a £20m animal testing research laboratory in Oxford."[299] Bizarre as it may seem, Broughton's "explosive substance" was sparklers: several explosive devices planted around Oxford used sparklers as part of their fuse, and when Broughton was arrested police found "14 packets of sparklers and a battery connector in an unused water tank in his bathroom."[300]

Denmark saw a final acquittal in a major case, where a 23-year-old Danish man of Turkish origin was accused of involvement in a terrorist plot. Though he had "posted messages on the Internet urging the kidnapping of Danish soldiers abroad"—seemingly in order to exchange them for Islamic militants who were jailed in Denmark—the court ruled that prosecutors could not prove that the messages were part of a terrorist conspiracy.[301]

There were also two mistrials in the United States. A federal jury was unable to reach a verdict in the case of the Liberty City Seven,

---

297. Aisha Iqbal, "Dewsbury Schoolboys 'Planned to Blow up the BNP,'" *Yorkshire Evening Post* (U.K.), Oct. 7, 2008.

298. "Teenage Bomb Plot Accused Cleared," *BBC News*, Oct. 23, 2008.

299. Owen Bowcott, "Animal Rights Activist Cleared of Sparklers Bomb Charge," *Guardian* (U.K.), Nov. 7, 2008.

300. Ibid.

301. "Danish Court Acquits Man in Soldier Kidnap Plot," *Fox News*, Nov. 18, 2008.

who were accused of taking part in a rather harebrained plot to bomb Chicago's Sears Tower. There was also a mistrial in the case of Naveed Haq, who opened fire in the offices of the Jewish Federation of Greater Seattle in July 2006—killing one and wounding five while he "railed against Jews and U.S. policies with Israel."[302] Haq's lawyers never contested the facts of the shooting, instead arguing that a change in his medication for mental maladies identified as "bipolar disorder with psychotic tendencies" had triggered the attack.[303] Mistrials are not necessarily defeats for the prosecution, as these cases can be brought to trial anew: in fact, prosecutors secured convictions in the Liberty City Seven case in 2009.

Appeals

As previously noted, several convictions were overturned on appeal due to evidentiary issues during the course of 2008.

In July, Spain's Supreme Court overturned the convictions of four people—Basel Ghalyoun, Mohamed Almallah Dabas, Abdelilah El Fadual El Akil, and Raul Gonzalez Pena—who had previously been found guilty of being involved in the country's notorious 2004 Madrid train bombings. The court found that there was insufficient evidence to support their convictions, although it did reverse the acquittal of Antonio Toro, and sentence him to four years for trafficking explosives.

The Spanish Supreme Court also overturned the convictions of fourteen of the twenty men convicted of playing roles in a 2004 plot to blow up Madrid's High Court. The Supreme Court ruled "that investigators based their case on insufficient evidence and that the High Court was wrong to find many of the suspects guilty."[304] Despite this, the court found that there was "without doubt" a terrorist plot against the High Court, and it upheld the conviction of group leader Abderrahmane Tahiri. The court noted that he was "'nearly obsessed' with his plan to kill Spanish judges by bombing the court building."[305]

In October, the United States Court of Appeals for the Second

---

302. Natalie Singer, "Mistrial Declared In Seattle Jewish Center Shooting Case," *Seattle Times*, June 5, 2008.
303. "Judge Declares Mistrial in Seattle Jewish Center Shooting Case" *Associated Press*, June 5, 2008.
304. "Spain Acquits 14 Accused Islamists," *El País* (Spain), Oct. 8, 2008.
305. "Spanish Court Quashes Bomb Plot Convictions," *Reuters*, Oct. 7, 2008.

Circuit overturned the convictions of defendants Mohammed Ali Al-Moayad and Mohammed Mohsen Zayed, who had been found guilty of conspiring to provide material support to Hamas and al-Qaeda. Their convictions were overturned after the Second Circuit found that the district court had committed prejudicial evidentiary errors.[306] The defendants remain in custody pending a new trial.

In the U.K. a set of convictions was overturned on purely legal grounds when five young Muslim students (four of whom were in their first year at Bradford University) who had been convicted "for downloading and sharing extremist terrorism-related material"[307] had their sentences overturned by the Court of Appeal. The four Bradford University students—Aitzaz Zafar, Usman Malik, Akbar Butt, and Awaab Iqbal—had become close to then-17-year-old Mohammed Raja in 2006 through exchanges over the Internet.[308] They had initially been convicted under Section 57 of the 2000 Terrorism Act, which provides that "[a] person commits an offence if he possesses an article in circumstances which give rise to a reasonable suspicion that his possession is for a purpose connected with the commission, preparation or instigation of an act of terrorism."

The Court of Appeal held that there had to be a "direct connection between the object possessed and the act of terrorism"—that the section should be interpreted as though it read: "A person commits an offence if he possesses an article in circumstances which give rise to a reasonable suspicion that he intends it to be used for the purpose of the commission, preparation or instigation of an act of terrorism."[309] Under this construction, the court held that the students' convictions could not stand because their use of the material was not related to planning terrorist acts. As the BBC reports, this could prove to be a highly significant decision in Britain because "there have been three other convictions under this legislation—more cases are expected before the courts this year."[310]

Imran Khan, the solicitor for one of the accused, expressed

---

306. *United States v. Moayed*, No. 05-4186-CR (2nd Cir. Oct. 2, 2008).
307. "Five Students Win Terror Appeal," *BBC News*, Feb. 13, 2008.
308. "Students Sentenced in Terror Case," *Independent* (U.K.), July 26, 2007.
309. *Zafar v. R*, 2008 EWCA Crim 184 (U.K. Court of Appeal, Criminal Division, Feb. 13, 2008), ¶ 29.
310. "Five Students Win Terror Appeal," *BBC News*.

the concerns of civil liberties advocates and many in the Muslim community: "Young Muslim men before this judgement could have been prosecuted simply for simply looking at any material on the basis that it might be connected in some way to terrorist purposes."[311]

Not all appeals were unsuccessful for the prosecution. The United States Court of Appeals for the Fourth Circuit upheld the conviction of Virginia Jihad Network member Ali Asad Chandia, although it did find that a new sentencing hearing was needed.[312] Similarly, the Second Circuit Court of Appeals upheld the conviction of Shahwar Matin Siraj, who had been convicted of plotting to set off a bomb in New York City's Herald Square subway station. Also, a British court upheld the convictions of five men accused of plotting a series of attacks using fertilizer bombs in Britain (although two of the defendants received reduced sentences).

LOGISTICAL SUPPORT FOR TERRORISM

Prosecutors experienced success in a range of cases during 2008 in which the defendants faced charges for providing logistical support or material support to the terrorist cause.

Terrorist Financing

Prosecutions against the financial backing and support of terrorist organizations serve as a pressure point designed to limit the expansion of terrorist networks. The landmark terrorist financing case in 2008 occurred in the United States, where prosecutors secured convictions in the Holy Land Foundation case. The Holy Land Foundation (HLF) and a number of its officials were accused of engaging in money laundering in support of the terrorist group Hamas, which has been responsible for a large number of attacks against Israeli civilians and other targets. During the late 1980s and into the 1990s, HLF openly provided support for Hamas, which was named a specially designated terrorist organization in 1995.[313] It also

---

311. Ibid.
312. *United States v. Chandia*, No. 06-4997 (4th Cir. Jan. 23, 2008).
313. *United States v. Holy Land Foundation for Relief and Development*, Indictment at 5, 8 (N.D. Tex., July 26, 2004).

sponsored a number of conferences and conventions featuring radical sheikhs and Hamas officials that were designed to help them raise funds; some events featured songs and skits depicting the killing of Jews.[314] After the Oslo Accords, which were designed to promote peace between Israel and the Palestinians, HLF's principals met with Hamas activists in Philadelphia to try to determine how HLF could support Hamas's "opposition to the peace plan and to decide how to conceal their activities from the scrutiny of the United States government."[315]

The first criminal trial against HLF for its support for Hamas resulted in a mistrial on October 22, 2007, after the jurors found themselves deadlocked on some of the charges.[316] The retrial occurred in 2008. This time, after six weeks of testimony and a week of deliberation, the jury found HLF and five of its officials guilty of providing material support to Hamas.[317]

Following the verdict, Matthew Levitt of the Washington Institute for Near East Policy, one of the U.S.'s foremost experts on Hamas, wrote:

> The message sent by the verdict in this case is clear: the United States will neither allow itself to be used as a cash-cow by terrorist groups raising money here under the guise of legitimate charitable activity nor will it allow such groups to abuse the charitable sector by fraudulently raising funds for purportedly innocent causes and then using those funds to finance terrorism.... Beyond this specific case, the verdict is also a very significant win coming as it does on the heels of several less successful attempts to prosecute individuals and organizations raising funds for Palestinian terrorist groups in this country. For example, in 2005, Sami al-Arian was acquitted on most charges in a similar case in Tampa, Florida, but then pled guilty to conspiracy in providing funds or services to Palestinian Islamic Jihad.

---

314. Ibid. at 8-9.
315. Ibid. at 9.
316. Leslie Eaton, "No Convictions in Trial Against Muslim Charity," *New York Times*, Oct. 22, 2007.
317. U.S. Department of Justice, Press Release, "Federal Jury in Dallas Convicts Holy Land Foundation and its Leaders for Providing Material Support to Hamas Terrorist Organization," Nov. 24, 2008.

Similarly, two men charged with financing Hamas were acquitted in a Chicago case earlier this year, but were convicted on lesser terrorism-related charges.[318]

A Singular Victory, However Pyrrhic to Some
by Jeff Breinholt

When it was announced in the fall of 2007 that the judge had declared a mistrial after the jury failed to reach a unanimous verdict in the Holy Land Foundation case—the most significant terrorist financing prosecution in American history—the public commentary was positively gleeful. The disconnect between spin and reality reminded of that famous headline in the Harvard Crimson, circa November 1968. "HARVARD DEFEATS YALE, 29-29," it proclaimed.

The *Washington Post* led the chorus, with a headline announcing that the Department of Justice had few wins to show for all of its efforts tracking terrorists over the previous eight years. The *Boston Globe* got into the act talking about other cases, as did *Rolling Stone* and *Mother Jones*.

It turns out rumors of the acquittal of the Holy Land Foundation principals were greatly exaggerated. When the retrial came around, the prosecutors, true professionals all, got busy again. The results were nothing to sneeze at: all of the Holy Land defendants were convicted of all charges. There was no acquittal. Last May, the judge sentenced them to between 15 and 20 years in prison. Not bad for a white-collar case.

This turn-about apparently does not satisfy the Department of Justice's critics. When the government loses, it is big news, and the verdict surely means something. The same is true when a jury fails to reach a verdict in the first go-round, as happened in the so-called Liberty City Seven case in Miami. Meanwhile, when the government wins, there is a palpable sense that it is not such a big deal. Critics come out of the woodwork, complaining that the verdict does not really signify guilt, that the cases took too much government resources (as if terrorist financiers are a minor nuisance), and that the government was wrong to choose this route. It is nihilism at its worst, and a maddening form of one-way myopia.

---

318. Matthew Levitt, "HLF Verdict: Guilty on All Counts," *Counterterrorism Blog*, Nov. 24, 2008.

What is ironic is that some of the most hardened critics of the law enforcement approach to terrorism are also the most aggressive critics of military tools. What do they think will happen if criminal prosecutions are scrubbed from the choice of options in dealing with international terrorism? That more kinetic tools—that is, military actions—will become less likely to be used?

What makes this rearguard action against law enforcement so pernicious—despite clear wins like the Holy Land Foundation case—is a perfect storm of critics on both ends of the political spectrum. On the right, there are critics who sneer at the very notion that terrorism is anything but a military problem, and by the sensible suggestion that we need to find a way to incapacitate those against whom military options are unavailable. On the left, there are those who view public accusations by the government—which, at the end of the day, must be backed by admissible evidence for the charges to stick—as an ideal vehicle to argue that the government is politicizing the judiciary, making stuff up, picking on the wrong culprits, and blindly siding with Israel. Each side has seemingly come together in an exhibit of information warfare, to great effect. No wonder criminal prosecutions of terrorists are drying up.

Probably the greatest misunderstanding driving this tendency is the myth that the government acts with one brain. In reality, there are a number of vital nerve centers that sent mixed signals to the Chief Executive. Is terrorism a military or law enforcement issue? The answer is yes—both. Persons within the government responsible for these respective tools should be encouraged to fight internal battles for the right to do what they do best. The President and his advisors must choose which option to exercise when. If criminal law is no longer an option, we have tied one of our hands behind our back, and only have ourselves to blame.

In the end, what was gained by the Holy Land Foundation case? For one, there was justice for those whose family members were killed by Hamas terrorism in the 1990s and 2000s, some several dozen people who saw their assailants' stateside fundraisers get their due. For another, there is a clear signal that, whatever the critics say, the criminal justice system can work in terrorism cases, and people can be punished for what they do with their money. Doubt that? Ask Martha Stewart. The ACLU and the Center for

Constitutional Rights have no trouble trying to extend liability to financiers who helped prop up the South African Apartheid regime or American companies that sell bulldozers to Israel. Applying the same standards to Palestinian terrorist organizations raises the "guilt by association" mantra.

To these positive results, I would add a third. Countries like the United States that have joined the U.N. Convention for the Suppression of Terrorist Financing (sponsored by France) have an obligation under international law to prosecute terrorist financing they uncover in their territories. That means that every U.S. terrorist financing prosecution is compelled by our multilateral commitments. In other words, these cases cannot be explained as a function of an ideological Executive Branch or wrong-headed American unilateralism. Terrorist financing prosecutions should occur irrespective of which party is in the White House, assuming the incumbent takes international commitments seriously. Currently, in terms of terrorist financing-related international obligations, we are the most compliant country in the world. If you are a multilateralist, you should not complain. Every time the U.S. announces an indictment of a terrorism financier, it is complying with its international obligations.

Finally, there is this tidbit: criminal prosecutions are nothing if not humanitarian, which is part of the reason conservatives have so lined up against it. Nobody is tortured in the courtroom, and— at least judging by the U.S. record in major terrorism cases—few defendants are given the death penalty. Sure, law enforcement cannot replace good old-fashioned boots on the ground, nor should it. However, it must remain a viable part of our counterterrorism arsenal. Fortunately, the Holy Land Foundation case serves as a reminder of that, no matter how pyrrhic the media would make it.

Also in the U.S., Pakistani national Saifullah Anjun Ranjha pleaded guilty to conspiring to launder money and concealing terrorist financing. Ranjha had been involved in operating a money-transfer business (*hawala*) in Washington, D.C., and according to the indictment against him he had transferred money for a cooperating witness who told him the funds would support al-Qaeda. This case is indicative of how law enforcement has adapted to an evolving terrorist financing environment, in that investigators have long suspected that bin Laden has used *hawalas* "to move money and finance the activities of his terrorist network."[319]

Sometimes supporters of terrorism determine that specific revenue streams will be used to finance terrorist groups. In this report's previous section, for example, we noted that the prevalence of crime within Bulgaria has created a space for terrorist fundraising activities. In September 2008, a Danish appellate court convicted six people of selling t-shirts to fund terrorist organizations—the Revolutionary Armed Forces of Colombia (FARC) and the Popular Front for the Liberation of Palestine.[320] This conviction reversed the initial decision of a district court that found group members not guilty in 2007.

Another revenue stream that has traditionally been used to fund terrorism is drug money. The major court case linking drug revenues to the financing of terrorism in 2008 occurred in the United States. On May 15, Khan Mohammed was convicted of narcotics distribution and narco-terrorism, "the distribution of a controlled substance (in this case heroin and opium) in order to provide something of pecuniary value to a person or group that has engaged or is engaging in terrorist activity."[321] Drug Enforcement Administration (DEA) agents working in Afghanistan were assisted by an Afghan farmer in capturing film of Mohammed inspecting packaged opium and heroin, which U.S. authorities believe was to be used to finance Taliban activities, and plotting to launch a rocket attack on a U.S. air base. According to video transcripts, Mohammed stated that "the Americans are infidels, and Jihad is allowed against them... If we have to fire toward the airport, we will do it, and if not the airport, wherever else they are stationed."[322] According to Bruce C. Swartz, Deputy Assistant Attorney General in the Justice Department's Criminal Division, Mohammed is the first person to be convicted of narco-terrorism since the offense was signed into

---

319. Ramond McCaffrey, "Dozens Charged in Money Sting," *Washington Post*, Sept. 21, 2007.
320. John Tagliabue, "Denmark: T-Shirt Sellers Convicted in Terrorism Case," *New York Times*, Sept.18, 2008.
321. U.S. Department of Justice, Press Release, "Member of Afghan Taliban Sentenced to Life in Prison in Nation's First Conviction on Narco-Terror Charges," May 15, 2008.
322. Del Quentin Wilber, "Afghan Farmer Helps Convict Taliban Member in U.S. Court," *Washington Post*, Dec. 23, 2008.

law in March 2006 as part of the reauthorization of the Patriot Act.[323] He was sentenced to life in prison.

In another narcoterrorism case, Afghani Bashir Noorzai was convicted of international narcotics trafficking in September. Noorzai had been a long-time associate of Afghanistan's Taliban.[324]

Other Material Support

Beyond financial support, individuals in the West have attempted to provide terrorist groups with other forms of support. In some instances, terrorist groups have received classified information, weapons, and other supplies. There were successful prosecutions in 2008 for these kinds of material support of terrorism. In the United States, Hassan Abujihaad, also known as Paul R. Hall, was found guilty in March of materially supporting terrorism because he passed sensitive information to Islamic extremists while serving as a signalman aboard the *U.S.S. Benfold.*

Abujihaad's illegal activities came to light when British police found a floppy disk containing classified Navy information during a raid of the home of Babar Ahmad of Azzam Publications.[325] Abujihaad had sent them one electronic document, for example, that "discussed, in considerable detail, the makeup of [Abujihaad's] Battle Group, each of its member ships, (including the *U.S.S. Benfold*, on which Abujihaad was then stationed), the specifications, assignments and missions of each ship, the Battle Group's planned movements, and included a drawing of the group's formation when it was to pass through the Straits of Hormuz."[326]

He had been involved in correspondence with Azzam Publications for some time, as an affidavit filed in the criminal case describes:

Recovered emails between Abujihaad and Azzam Publications include discussions regarding: (1) videos

323. Bruce C. Swartz, Testimony Before the House Subcommittee on National Security and Foreign Affairs, June 18, 2008. For the narcoterrorism legislation, see 21 U.S.C. § 960a.
324. U.S. Attorney's Office, Southern District of New York, Press Release, "Top Taliban Associate and Former Mujahideen Warlord Found Guilty of Heroin Trafficking," Sept. 23, 2008.
325. "Former U.S. Navy Sailor Arrested on Terror Charges," *CNN*, Mar. 8, 2007.
326. *United States v. Abujihaad*, Indictment (D. Conn. Mar. 21, 2007), ¶ 23.

Abujihaad ordered from Azzam Publications that promoted violent jihad; (2) a small donation of money Abujihaad made to Azzam; and (3) whether it was "safe" to send materials to Abujihaad at his military address on board the *U.S.S. Benfold*. In another email, Abujihaad: (1) describes a recent force protection briefing given on board his ship; (2) voices enmity towards America; (3) praises Usama bin Laden and the mujahideen; (4) praises the October 2000 attack on the *U.S.S. Cole*; and (5) advises the members of Azzam Publications that such tactics are working and taking their toll. The response from Azzam Publications encourages Abujihaad to "keep up the psychological warefare" [sic].[327]

A British court also convicted five men of providing various kinds of logistical support for London's 7/21 bombing, as well as failing to disclose information to authorities about the plot, which occurred on July 21, 2005. The defendants were Abdul Waxid Sherif, Siraj Ali, Wahbi Mohammed, Muhedin Ali and Ismail Abdurahman. A Metropolitan Police bulletin explained how the five men had assisted 7/21 bombers Muktar Said Ibrahim, Hussain Osman, Yassin Omar, Manfo Asiedu and Ramzi Mohammed:

> Handwritten notes relating to the construction of the bombs used on 21/7 were found in Ali's flat and after the failed attacks he helped Ibrahim by clearing out the latter's property from his own flat at no. 65.... Wahbi Mohamed is the brother of Ramzi Mohammed (the Oval bomber). He was present at 14k Dalgarno Gardens, W10 on the morning of 21 July before the bombers prepared to set off to carry out the attacks. He took possession of a video camera—believed to have been used to make the bombers' suicide videos at Dalgarno Gardens—and also took Ramzi Mohammed's suicide letter intended for his family. After the attacks he helped Ramzi Mohammed by taking him food and other items as Ramzi remained in hiding with Ibrahim at Dalgarno Gardens. Muhedin Ali was a friend of Hussein Osman, Ramzi Mohammed and Wahbi Mohammed. After the attacks he offered Osman

---

327. Affidavit of FBI Special Agent David G. Dillon (D. Conn., Mar. 1, 2007), ¶ 21.

a safe-house in London and following Ali's arrest police discovered Ramzi Mohammed's suicide note. Ismail Abdurahman provided Hussain Osman with a safe-house after the attacks.[328]

Abdul Waxid Sherif received a jail term of ten years, Siraj Yassin Abdullah Ali twelve years, Wahbi Mohammed seventeen years, Muhedin Ali seven years, and Ismail Abdurahman ten years.

Four other people were convicted for assisting the 7/21 plotters and withholding information from authorities in June. Yeshi Girma, the wife of 7/21 plotter Hussain Osman, was convicted along with her brother Esayas, sister Mula, and sister's boyfriend Mohamed Kabashi. In a separate trial, Yassin Omar's fiancée Fardosa Abdullahi was convicted for helping the 7/21 plotter escape the day after the failed explosions.[329]

However, the trial of Waheed Ali, Sadeer Saleem and Mohammed Shakil, charged with assisting the 7/7 bombers, was halted after the jury could not reach a verdict; the retrial was scheduled for 2009.

In Australia, Belal Saadallah Khazaal was found guilty on September 10 of "making a document in connection with the engagement of a person in a terrorist act."[330] This verdict marked the first time someone had been convicted of the charge in an Australian court. The 110-page manual that Khazaal made, also referred to as a "do-it-yourself terrorism guide," covered a range of topics, such as "various means of assassination, including letterbombs, booby-trapping cars, kidnappings, poisonings, attacking motorcades and shooting down planes."[331]

328. Metropolitan Police (London), Bulletin 823, "Five Jailed for Assisting Terrorists," Feb. 4, 2008.

329. John-Paul Ford Rojas, "Woman Who Helped Failed Bomber is Jailed," *Independent* (U.K.), July 12, 2008.

330. Attorney-General's Department, Government of Australia, "Counter-Terrorism and Related Cases," Sept. 22, 2008.

331. Natalie O'Brien, "Belal Saadallah Khazaal Convicted for 'Terror Manual,'" *Australian*, Sept. 11, 2008.

TERRORIST PROPAGANDA AND RECRUITMENT

Terrorist propaganda and recruitment are two sides of the same coin. Propaganda is designed to win "hearts and minds" to the terrorists' cause, while recruitment goes a step further and actually attempts to entice people to be involved in terrorist operations.

Propaganda

Terrorist propaganda prosecutions were largely successful in 2008, with two notable setbacks on appeal. In the United States, Javed Iqbal and Saleh Elahwal pled guilty in late December to providing material support to a terrorist organization through his operations of a satellite television distribution company that illegally provided access to Al Manar broadcasts in the United States. Al Manar, Arabic for "the Beacon," is a television station based in Lebanon "that is designed to cultivate support for Hizballah's activities and mission. Through its broadcasts on Al Manar, Hizballah endeavors, among other things, to raise money for its activities and to recruit volunteers for future attacks."[332] As part of his plea agreement, Iqbal admitted that he was paid thousands of dollars by Al Manar in exchange for his satellite transmissions of the television station.[333]

Ibrahim Raschid, an Iraqi Kurdish political refugee who came to Germany in 1996, was convicted in June of twenty-two counts of terrorist solicitation and recruitment related to his propaganda efforts. The court found that Raschid had posted al-Qaeda videos on the Internet, including footage of Osama bin Laden calling for attacks on the West.[334] In his decision, Judge Wolfgang Siolek argued that by spreading these messages, Raschid was "a multiplier in the service of" the terrorist group.[335] Furthermore, Judge Siolek noted

that a primary aim of the defendant [Raschid] had been

---

332. *United States v. Iqbal*, Indictment, No. S1-06-Cr.-1054, June 20, 2007, ¶ 2.
333. U.S. Attorney's Office, Southern District of New York, Press Release, "Staten Island Satellite TV Operator Pleads Guilty to Providing Material Support to Hizballah TV Station," Dec. 23, 2008.
334. "Iraqi Jailed in Germany for Recruiting Terrorists Online," *Deutsche Welle* (Germany), June 19, 2008.
335. "Iraqi Convicted for Spreading al-Qaeda Messages on Web," *USA Today*, June 19, 2008.

to win over new members or supporters for al-Qaeda, although it could not be proven that he had actually succeeded. He said that the man's extremist views also had become clear in tapped telephone conversations with relatives in Iraq.[336]

The defense had contended that Raschid had only posted widely available videos and was not actively recruiting members; an argument the court refused to accept, in part because Raschid had supplemented the videos with his own commentary.[337] Raschid was the first person convicted in Germany under the new law that banned recruitment for terror organizations.[338]

There were two major convictions in Britain in 2008 related to terrorist propaganda. Abu Izzadeen (Trevor Brooks) and Simon Keeler were found guilty and sentenced to four and a half years imprisonment in April on charges of inciting people to commit overseas acts of terrorism and fundraising for terrorist organizations.[339] The pair had delivered a series of inflammatory speeches at London's Regents Park Mosque. The British press reported on the content of these speeches:

> While western troops were fighting in Fallujah in Nov 2004 the group delivered a series of speeches at the mosque boasting that they were terrorists and exhorting followers to give donations to buy arms for the holy war in Iraq.... The court heard that in another speech, recorded two years later in Birmingham, Brooks asked his audience: "Are you ready for another 7/7?" Keeler meanwhile, told listeners at the Regents Park Mosque: "Give your money to Osama Bin Laden, give your money to the Mujahideen. Go there physically and fight. Come fight the jihad. Islam will dominate the world, inevitable."[340]

Prosecutors held—and the court agreed—that the defendants had "crossed the line" beyond mere freedom of expression by actually

---

336. Ibid.
337. "Iraqi Jailed in Germany for Recruiting Terrorists Online," *Deutsche Welle.*
338. Ibid.
339. Metropolitan Police (London), Bulletin 843, "Six Men Convicted of Terrorism Offences," Apr. 17, 2008.
340. Duncan Gardham, "Muslim Preacher Abu Izzadeen Guilty of Inciting Terrorism," *Telegraph* (U.K.), Apr. 18, 2008.

encouraging their followers to join the jihad in Iraq.

A second British case of encouraging terrorism involved an individual who was motivated not by ideology, but rather by what the prosecution dubbed a "festering grudge." In February, Malcolm Hodges pled guilty to recklessly encouraging terrorism. He had sent numerous letters to mosques, claiming to be a follower of Osama bin Laden, and encouraging them to focus their jihad on "[t]he Institute of Chartered Accountants in England and Wales, the Association of Chartered Certified Accountants (ACCA), the Chartered Institute of Management Accountants and the Chartered Institute of Public Finance Accountants."[341] In his letters, Hodges argued that these institutions embodied "the corrupt and Western society which are abhorrent to true believers, which the infidels, in their arrogance, will not expect to be attacked." Moreover, he tried to phrase his call for jihad in a manner that might appeal to potential terrorists:

> Brothers, striking at these targets will be striking at the infidels where it hurts most and each of these targets was formed and is led by the Queen of England.... These targets are also full of swine and apes as they are crammed full of Jews, so striking against these targets is a strike against Israel and will take us closer to wiping Israel from the map.[342]

Hodges's grudge against the ACCA, and the accounting industry as a whole, stemmed from his failure to pass an accounting exam in the late 1990s. According to the prosecution, Hodges issued a number of threats toward the ACCA, leading them to increase security, and had written letters to the British Royal Family, the Prime Minister, and the Chancellor hoping to gain retribution for the "grave injustice" that had befallen him.[343]

During the sentencing, Judge Jeremy Roberts highlighted the seriousness of Hodges's actions: "There was a real risk that if one of your letters had fallen into the wrong hands there might have been a terrorist atrocity and people might have been killed or seriously

---

341. "Man Urged Terror Attacks on Accountancy Institutes," *Daily Mail* (U.K.), Feb. 19, 2008.
342. Ibid.
343. "'Jihad on Accountants' Man Jailed," *BBC News*, Feb. 19, 2008.

injured."[344] Hodges was sentenced to two years in prison.

However, two propaganda convictions were overturned on appeal in 2008. In one of these, a British appellate court overturned the 2007 conviction of Samina Malik for possessing articles "likely to be useful to a person committing or preparing an act of terrorism": police claimed that they found "a 'library' of extreme Islamist literature in her bedroom including The Al-Qaeda Manual and The Mujahideen Poisons Handbook."[345] A self-described "lyrical terrorist," Malik also posted poems in support of jihad on her website. While Malik argued that her poems were "meaningless" and that she only adopted her moniker "because it sounded cool," prosecutor Jonathan Sharp insisted: "These communications strongly indicate Samina Malik was deeply involved with terrorist related groups."[346]

In overturning Malik's conviction, the chief justice argued that jury was likely confused over what the exact crime was, a fact the prosecution conceded. The judgment stated:

> We do not consider that it was made plain to the jury, whether by the prosecution or by the Recorder, that the case that the appellants had to face was that they possessed the extremist material for use in the future to incite the commission of terrorist acts. We doubt whether the evidence supported such a case.

Sue Hemming, head of the counterterrorism division in the Crown Prosecution Service (CPS), noted that while the ruling meant Malik's poems "would no longer be held capable of giving practical assistance to terrorists," the other terrorist literature captured in Malik's home could allow for a retrial. (She did allow that given the time Malik spent in remand prior to the trial and the time served in her suspended sentence, CPS would not seek a retrial.)

An appellate court also overturned the convictions in Austria's first "homegrown" terrorism case, and ordered a retrial. In the case, a husband and wife (married under Islamic law but not Austria's civil code) were initially convicted on terrorism charges in March. The pair,

344. "Man Urged Terror Attacks on Accountancy Institutes," *Daily Mail.*
345. "'Lyrical Terrorist' Found Guilty," *BBC News*, Nov. 8, 2007.
346. Ibid.

identified in the media as Mohamed M. and Mona S., was convicted of "belonging to a terrorist organization, trying to blackmail the Austrian government and inciting a crime."[347] The terror group in question was the Global Islamic Media Front. However, Austria's highest court ordered a retrial in August.[348]

Mohamed M. was the more active of the two online. Evidence before the court described his activities:

> The Egyptian-born man, Mohamed M., was found guilty on charges of being involved in a March 2007 video that threatened to target Austria and Germany with terrorist attacks if they did not immediately withdraw their troops from Afghanistan. "In standing by the United States ... you have provoked those whom you call terrorists to target you," said the voice on the film as German and Austrian flag appeared against a burning background. [He] was also charged with threatening to target the European Championships soccer tournament, jointly hosted this June by Austria and Switzerland, and European politicians on radical Islamic Internet forums.[349]

Mona S. had primarily assisted Mohamed M.'s online activities; for example, by providing translation services.

Recruitment

There were three major successful prosecutions of terrorist recruitment in European courts in 2008. All four involved recruitment for the jihad in Iraq.

On January 10, Bilal Soughir was convicted in a Belgian court of belonging to a terrorist organization that sent fighters to Iraq.[350] Four accomplices were also convicted in absentia. Among the individuals

---

347. "Pair Sentenced for Terrorist Threat to Austria, Germany," *Deutsche Welle* (Germany), Mar. 13, 2008.
348. The February 2009 retrial subsequently found both defendants guilty, and sentenced them to five years in prison. "Vienna Terror Suspects Get 5 Years Jail," *Austrian Times*, Feb. 13, 2009.
349. "Pair Sentenced for Terrorist Threat to Austria, Germany."
350. "5 Men in Belgium Guilty of Sending Fighters to Iraq, Including Female Homicide Bomber," *Fox News*, Jan. 10, 2008.

that the network sent to Iraq was Muriel Degauque, the first European female suicide bomber to die in that country. Soughir received a sentence of ten years imprisonment.[351]

On May 14, a Parisian court convicted seven men, five of whom were French citizens, of "criminal association with a terrorist enterprise" for their roles in the recruitment and transport of young men to join al-Qaeda in Iraq.[352] Investigators asserted that the group sent "about a dozen Muslims to camps linked to al-Qaeda."[353] The individuals were all members of the 19th Arrondissement Cell, named after the low-income neighborhood where they lived and conducted their operations. Cell leader Farid Benyettou, whom Judge Jacqueline Rebeyrotte labeled "the ideologue" of the group, was sentenced to six years. The remaining individuals received sentences ranging from four to seven years. This was the first of two successful prosecutions in France for terrorist recruitment activity: in November, four members of the "Montpellier Cell" were found guilty of trying to send fighters to Iraq (although they were also convicted of plotting attacks in Italy and North Africa).[354]

MEMBERSHIP IN A TERRORIST ORGANIZATION

In some countries, it is illegal to be a member of a proscribed terrorist group. Frequently membership charges will be brought along with more significant terrorist offenses.

In Britain, Rangzieb Ahmed and Habib Ahmed were convicted in December of being members of al-Qaeda. As with many of the Islamic terror prosecutions that occurred over the course of 2008, the plot had significant links back to Pakistan. Raffaello Pantucci, a research associate at the International Institute for Strategic Studies, notes that the case was significant in part because "it further showed the depth of interconnectedness between British extremist networks and al-

---

351. Julien Ponthus, "Belgian Court Jails Iraq Suicide Bomb Recruiters," *Reuters,* Jan. 10, 2008.
352. "Paris Court Convicts 7 on Terror Charges," *USA Today,* May 14, 2008.
353. "French Iraq Recruiters are Jailed," *BBC News,* May 14 2008.
354. "Men Jailed over Jihad Plans," *Reuters*, Nov. 7, 2008.

Qaeda's core in Pakistan."[355] Mehreen Haji, Habib's wife, was cleared of two terrorist financing counts.

UNDERCHARGING

One significant trend in recent years in terrorism prosecutions has been undercharging—charging people suspected of serious terrorist offenses with lesser crimes than what might have been brought against them. As per John Ashcroft's explanation of the "Al Capone model" for terrorism prosecutions, the advantage is that prosecutors will be able to earn convictions of individuals suspected of terrorist activity when they may not have all the evidence necessary to win convictions based on terrorism charges. One disadvantage to this style of prosecution is that those who are convicted will receive shorter prison sentences; and it may also make it more difficult for the public to understand the actual magnitude of the terrorist threat.

One case of undercharging occurred, in Australia, where Jack Thomas, also known as "Jihad Jack," was sentenced to nine months imprisonment on October 29 for possessing a falsified passport. Thomas had converted to Islam at the age of twenty-three, after exploring various other religions.[356] He chose Jihad as his Muslim name following his conversion. Thomas traveled to Afghanistan in March 2001 to fight alongside the Taliban in the country's civil war. While attempting to return to Australia in 2003, he was detained in Pakistan and held for six months without charge. He was interrogated during that time by Pakistani, American, and Australian officials. Ultimately Thomas was returned to Australia, where he faced trial on terrorism charges. Though he was initially convicted of accepting money and a plane ticket from an al-Qaeda agent, Thomas's conviction was quashed by an appellate court that found some of the evidence used against him—including a March 2003 interview with AFP—inadmissible.[357] However, Thomas gave a subsequent interview in which he openly admitted to falsifying his passport, and the interview gave the prosecution grounds to argue for a retrial, which occurred in 2008.

---

355. Raffaello Pantucci, "U.K. Trial Exposes al-Qaeda Terrorist Network with Connections to Pakistan," *Terrorism Monitor*, The Jamestown Foundation, Jan. 23, 2009.
356. Henry Schuster, "The Story of Jihad Jack," *CNN*, Mar. 3, 2006.
357. "Jack Thomas Found Not Guilty of Receiving al-Qaeda Funds," *Adelaide Now* (Australia), Oct. 23, 2008.

The retrial was a textbook case of undercharging, in that Thomas was suspected of far greater offenses than passport falsification. He was convicted on charges that carried a maximum sentence of two years; since Thomas had already spent five years in detention, he was immediately released.[358]

Another case of undercharging occurred in the U.S., with the case against Care International. The Islamic charity Care International, according to prosecutors, had been involved in a range of jihadist activity:

> Evidence presented during the 24-day trial proved that the defendants fraudulently used Care International to solicit and obtain tax deductible donations for the purpose of supporting and promoting the mujahideen (Muslim holy warriors) and jihad (violent armed conflict).... Care International was an outgrowth of and successor to the Al-Kifah Refugee Center ("Al-Kifah") and was engaged in non-charitable activities involving the solicitation and expenditure of funds to support and promote the mujahideen and jihad from the IRS, FBI, and Immigration and Naturalization Service (now known as Immigration and Customs Enforcement).[359]

However, three former Care International officers were not charged with terrorism offenses, but rather with engaging in a scheme to conceal material facts from the U.S. and conspiring to defraud the U.S. In particular, Care International had claimed that it was granted tax-exempt status when this was not the case.

---

358. "Jack Thomas Freed after Five-Year Ordeal," *Australian*, Oct. 29, 2008.
359. U.S. Department of Justice, Press Release, "Former Officers of a Muslim Charity, CARE International, Inc., Convicted," Jan. 11, 2008.

ABOUT THE AUTHORS

The Authors

DAVEED GARTENSTEIN-ROSS

Daveed Gartenstein-Ross is the vice president of research at the Foundation for Defense of Democracies (FDD), and the director of its Center for Terrorism Research (CTR). He co-authored CTR's monograph *Homegrown Terrorists in the U.S. and U.K.: An Empirical Examination of the Radicalization Process*, which was published by FDD Press in April 2009. Gartenstein-Ross is a Ph.D. candidate in world politics at the Catholic University of America, and earned a J.D. from the New York University School of Law.

JOSHUA D. GOODMAN

Joshua D. Goodman is the director of research at FDD, and the deputy director of CTR. Goodman's research focuses on Iranian and Persian Gulf affairs, Israeli and inter-Arab politics, and transnational security issues. He earned a B.A. (honors) in history from York University (Toronto), and M.A. (magna cum laude) in Middle Eastern History from Tel Aviv University.

LAURA GROSSMAN

Laura Grossman is a research analyst at CTR. She received a bachelor's degree in history from the University of Michigan, and a M.S. in global affairs from New York University. She co-authored *Homegrown Terrorists in the U.S. and U.K.* with Daveed Gartenstein-Ross. At NYU, Grossman was a founding member and managing editor of *Perspectives on Global Issues*, the first student-run publication at NYU's Center for Global Affairs.

The Contributors

JEFF BREINHOLT

Jeff Breinholt, a 19-year Department of Justice veteran, is the author of three books and several dozen articles on national security and intelligence. He is a Lecturer in Law at George Washington University Law School. The views he expresses in this report are his own, and do not represent those of the Department of Justice.

DOUGLAS FARAH

Douglas Farah is a senior fellow at the International Assessment and Strategy Center. He co-authored *Merchant of Death: Money, Guns, Planes and the Man Who Makes War Possible* (Wiley, 2007), the definitive account of Viktor Bout. For two decades, Farah was a foreign correspondent and investigative reporter for the *Washington Post, UPI,* and other publications.

ROHAN GUNARATNA

Rohan Gunaratna is the head of the International Centre for Political Violence and Terrorism Research, Institute of Defence and Strategic Studies in Singapore. He holds a masters degree in international peace studies from Notre Dame, where he was Hesburgh Scholar, and a doctorate in international relations from St Andrews, where he was British Chevening Scholar. Gunaratna has over 20 years of academic, policy, and operational experience in counterterrorism, and has written several books about the LTTE.

ANDREW C. MCCARTHY

Andrew C. McCarthy is a senior fellow at the National Review Institute, a contributing editor at *National Review*, and author of the national bestseller *Willful Blindness: A Memoir of the Jihad* (Encounter Books, 2008). He is co-chairman of the Center for Law & Counterterrorism at the Foundation for Defense of Democracies. For 18 years, McCarthy was an Assistant United States Attorney in the Southern District of New York, and led the terrorism prosecution against Sheikh Omar Abdel Rahman and eleven others in connection with the 1993 World Trade Center bombing and a plot to bomb New York City landmarks. In his final five years at the Justice Department, he was the Chief Assistant U.S. Attorney of the Southern District's satellite office in White Plains. McCarthy is the recipient of numerous awards, including the Justice Department's highest honors: the Attorney General's Exceptional Service Award and the Attorney General's Distinguished Service Award.

REUVEN PAZ

Reuven Paz is the founder of the Project for the Research of Islamist Movements (PRISM) in the GLORIA Center at the Interdisciplinary Center, Herzliya, Israel, which he directs. He is fluent in written and spoken Arabic. Most of Paz's studies, research, and experience for the past 30 years have focused on Islamic culture, Islamic radicalism, and development of radical Islamic doctrines throughout the world. In 2006, PRISM opened a special research project focusing on radical Islam in Africa.

www.ingramcontent.com/pod-product-compliance
Lightning Source LLC
Chambersburg PA
CBHW081418270326
41931CB00015B/3322